Carpentry

AN INTRODUCTION TO SAWING, DRILLING, SHAPING & JOINING WOOD

COOL
SPRINGS
PRESS
Home and Garden Experts™

MINNEAPOLIS, MINNESOTA

CONTENTS

Tools, Materials & Skills

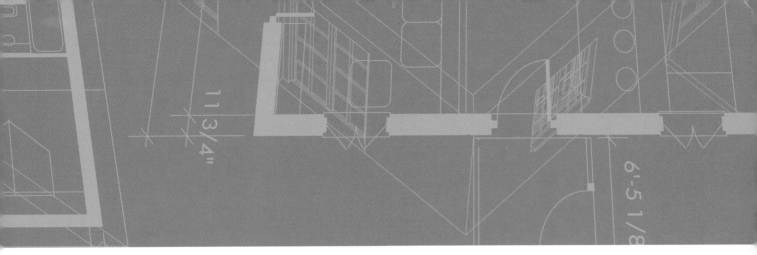

Basic Carpentry

Workshop

Anatomy of a House

References

Introduction

FUNDAMENTAL CARPENTRY SKILLS are a real must-have for anyone who wants to be moderately self-sufficient. On the easy end are the projects that stump so many but are so rudimentary—assembling a pre-fab shelving unit, hanging artwork, or easing a stuck door. With your collection of basic carpentry tools and an understanding of how to use them correctly, you will know which tool to use, how to locate studs, and how to sand or plane a door so it stops sticking.

Beyond the basics is a whole world of carpentry that you can do yourself. From birdhouses, doghouses, and sheds to your own house, knowing how to measure, cut, shape, assemble, and secure lumber, trim, and sheet goods is priceless. Even if you never attempt a major construction project like building partition walls, it is beneficial to know what the skeleton of your home looks like.

Throughout the book are Skillbuilder exercises. These are little activities to help you learn how to use a tool or material. If you didn't spend your childhood in the garage experimenting with every piece of scrap wood and every tool, you need to spend some playtime experimenting and developing skills. The more you practice on small projects, the better your big, serious projects will turn out. Remember, you may need to experience failure with tools and materials to understand how to achieve success.

Homeskills: Carpentry is a valuable resource on your road to self-reliance. Here you will find all the most common carpentry tools—photographs so you know what they look like, buying tips so you know what to look for, and technique tips to perfect your methodology. Use this book as a launch point to adventures in home repair and home improvem-ent, or use it as a handy reference to augment your hardware knowledge.

TOOLS, MATERIALS & SKILLS

You absolutely do not need pneumatic tools to be a home carpenter—but don't let them intimidate you. They are actually a lot of fun to use.

IF YOU WANT YOUR PROJECTS TO LOOK THEIR

best, they need to be level, plumb, true, and square. Achieving this state requires the proper tools—and attention to detail. Fortunately, measuring tools are some of the least expensive tools to purchase. At minimum, your toolbox should contain a tape measure, torpedo level, and a Speed square, and probably a studfinder. Plumb bobs and chalklines are necessary for framing and other larger construction jobs. Longer levels and various types of squares will come in handy as you build your skills.

Cutting accurately is as important as measuring accurately. A variety of hand and power tools are available to cut and shape wood. The circular saw is a power tool that most home carpenters should own. A good hand saw or two can also come in handy. Both power miters and table saws get less expensive every year.

Of course, once cut, all that lumber needs to be assembled. Hammers and power drills/drivers are also on the must-have list. Not all hammers are created the same, so we show you what to look for.

When acquiring your tool collection, purchase the highest quality you can afford. Sure, those hundred-piece tool kits for $19.99 are a great deal, but are they a good value? When the screwdriver bends on the first hard twist or the hammerhead flies off the handle on the first dry day, you will wish you had spent a bit more wisely.

One way to economize is to look for used tools at garage sales. Many hand tools have a lifespan of decades, and many older tools were built to last. For power tools, look for reconditioned models offered by the manufacturer. If you have handy relatives, they might be an excellent resource for secondhand tools. Many do-it-yourselfers upgrade their tools regularly. They may be happy to give you their old torpedo level if you ask.

Demolition is an important part of many carpentry projects. And just like building, it's all about the tools.

A quality prying tool is an essential part of any homeowner's tool kit. A flat prybar like the one seen here (sometimes called a wonderbar) is a very useful tool.

PRYING TOOLS

Prying tools are an essential part of any carpenter's tool arsenal, because many carpentry projects start with the removal of existing materials. With the right tools, you can often remove nails without damaging the lumber, so that it can be used again.

Pry bars are available in many sizes. Choose quality pry bars forged from high-carbon steel in a single piece. Most pry bars have a curved claw at one end for pulling nails and a chisel-shaped tip at the opposite end for other prying jobs. You can improve leverage by placing a wood block an inch or two away from the material you're trying to pry loose.

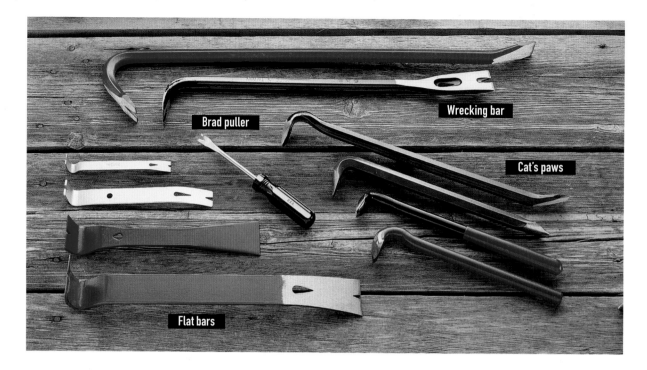

Prying tools include wrecking bars for heavy demolition work, cat's paws for removing nails, and a brad puller. Flat bars are made of flattened steel and come in a variety of sizes for light- and heavy-duty use.

Use the right tool for the job. A wrecking bar, sometimes called a crowbar, is a rigid tool for demolition and heavy prying jobs. As its name implies, it is good for wrecking. If you are removing trim, use a thin, flat pry bar. The claw on a claw hammer is meant for light-duty nail removal. If you will be pulling many nails, use a one piece flat bar or cat's paw so you don't ruin your hammer.

A cat's paw has a sharpened claw for removing stubborn nails. Use a hammer to drive the claw into the wood under the nail head, then lever the tool to pull up the nail.

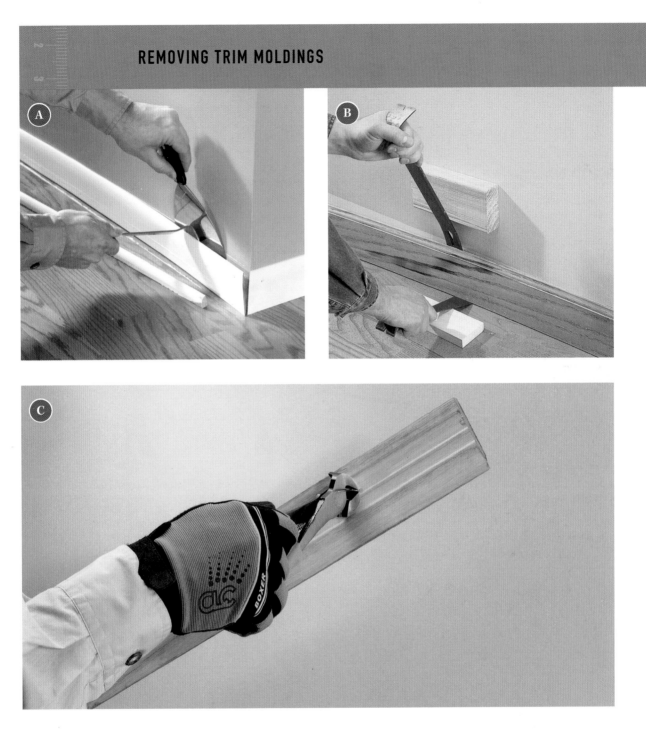

A   Trim moldings are often layered composites. Begin by removing the base shoe or outermost layer first. Use a wide drywall or putty knife to initiate the prying and make room for a flat pry bar.

B   Use large flat scraps of wood to protect wall and floor surfaces from damage. For base trim, which may be nailed both into the wall and the floor, insert one bar beneath the trim and work the other between the base and the wall. Force the pry bars in opposing directions to work the molding away from the wall.

C   Remove nails from trim by using an end nippers to grab the pointed end of the nail and pull the nail through the back side of the trim. This causes the least amount of damage to the front face of the trim. Use the rounded head of the end nippers to "roll" the nail out of the molding.

TAPE MEASURES

The first step in any carpentry project is the taking of accurate measurements. Even though it seems big, buy a 25-foot steel tape measure with a ¾-inch-wide blade for general use. Most tape measures are retractable, so the tape returns easily. Make sure your tape has a locking mechanism, so you can keep it extended to a desired length. A belt clip is also essential.

Wider tapes normally have a longer standout—the distance a tape can be extended before it bends under its own weight. A long standout is an extremely useful feature when you're measuring without a partner to support the far end of the tape. Open a tape in the store and extend it until it bends. It should have a standout of at least 7 feet.

Tape measures are commonly set in ¹⁄₁₆-inch increments along the top edge and ¹⁄₃₂-inch increments for the first six inches across the bottom. Select one with numbers that are easy to read. "Easy reader" tapes feature a fractional readout for people who have difficulty reading a measurement calibrated with dash marks. Most tape measures feature numbers that are marked or labeled every 16 inches for easy marking of studs. A high-quality tape measure also has a two- or three-rivet hook to control the amount of play in the tape, ensuring your measurements are as accurate as possible.

Buy a 25-ft. retractable steel tape for general carpentry projects. If you are working on a large project like a deck, patio, or retaining wall, consider purchasing a 50-ft. reel-type tape.

Skillbuilder

The end hook on a tape measure has between $\frac{1}{16}$ and $\frac{1}{8}$" of play so that the hook pushes in for taking an inside measurement and pulls out for taking an outside edge measurement. The hook end should not be used when an extremely accurate measurement is required. For precise measurements, use the 1" mark as your starting point (called burying an inch), then subtract 1" from your reading. Using the hook end, measure 5" from the end of a board. Then measure by burying an inch (shown).

Use only one tape measure, if possible, while working on a project. If you must work with two tapes, make sure they record the same measurement. Different tape measures do not always measure equally. A slight difference in the end hooks can create an error of $\frac{1}{16}$" or more between two tapes, even if they are of the same brand and style.

Check for square when building frames, boxes, cabinets, drawers, and other projects where fit is important. Hold a tape measure across the diagonals of the workpiece (A-C, B-D). The measurements will be identical if the workpiece is square.

PLUMB BOBS, CHALK LINES & STUD FINDERS

The plumb bob is a simple, yet extremely precise tool used to establish a line that is plumb—or exactly vertical. Plumb bobs are commonly used to find marking points to position a sole plate when building a wall. Plumb refers to a hypothetical line running to the exact center of the earth. Think of it as a line that is exactly perpendicular to a level surface.

The chalk line is a tool used to mark straight lines on flat surfaces for layout or to mark sheet goods and lumber for cutting. Typical chalk lines contain 50 to 100 feet of line wound up in a case filled with chalk. Always tap the box lightly to fully coat the line with chalk before pulling it out. To mark a line, extend it from the case, pull it taut, and snap it using the thumb and forefinger. Chalk lines have a crank that is used to reel in the line when the job is complete and a locking mechanism to help keep the line taut during marking.

Most of today's chalk lines (sometimes called chalk boxes) double as plumb bobs for general use (see photos, opposite page, bottom). A chalk box isn't quite as accurate as a plumb bob for establishing a vertical line. However, if you don't own a plumb bob, using a chalk box is an easy alternative.

Studfinders are battery-powered electronic devices that analyze wall density. They can help you locate wall framing and even electrical wires, depending on the model.

Buy powdered chalk refills of blue or red chalk. In most cases blue is a better choice because it is less permanent. Red is used mostly by professionals whose lines need to be visible for inspectors.

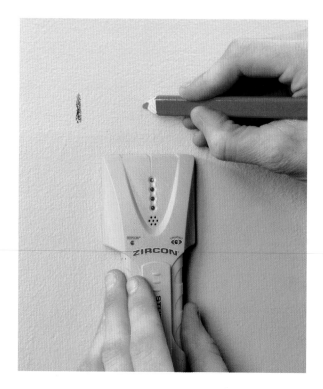

Use a studfinder to locate wall studs or ceiling blocking. These devices locate the edges of framing so you can determine the center of studs and joists.

Tip
When driving nails or screws into studs, the fastener must not penetrate more than 1" into the stud. Why? Electrical and plumbing lines run through the middle of studs. The finish layer of drywall is ½" thick on walls, so a 1¼" fastener is the safest length.

Skillbuilder

Practice this skill in a closet, finished garage, or basement where rows of holes won't be noticed. Use the studfinder to find a stud. Mark the edges of the stud, then confirm framing locations by driving a finish nail through the wall in a line between and beyond the marks. To find neighboring studs, measure from the center point of the confirmed stud in 16" or 24" intervals. Use the nail to verify. This exercise also acquaints you with the feeling of driving a nail through wall finish into a stud (good) or through wall finish into air (bad).

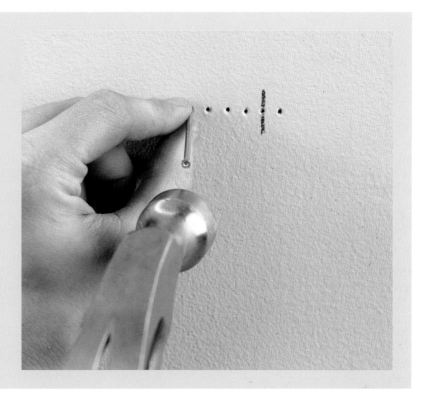

To snap a chalk line over a very short distance, pin the string down with the edge of your palm, then use your thumb and forefinger on the same hand to snap the line. When snapping lines to mark stud locations, make sure you snap over the center of the studs, so you will know where to drive screws or nails.

To position a sole plate, hang a plumb bob (or chalk box, as shown) from the edge of the top plate so that it nearly touches the floor. When it hangs motionless, mark the floor directly below the point of the plumb bob. Repeat the process at each end of the new wall space to determine the proper sole plate position.

LEVELS

Levels are essential to virtually every carpentry project. They help you build walls that are perfectly vertical (plumb), shelves, countertops, steps that are level, and roofs that incline at a correct and consistent pitch.

Take care of your levels. Unlike some other tools that can be tossed into a tool bucket without damage, a level is a finely tuned instrument that is easily broken. Before you buy a level, test it on a level surface to make sure the vials are accurate (opposite page).

Most levels contain one or more bubble gauges—sealed vials with a single small air bubble suspended in fluid—that indicate the level's orientation in space at any moment. As the level is tilted, the bubble shifts its position inside the vial to reflect the change. This type of level is sometimes referred to as a spirit level because of the use of alcohol inside the gauge. There are also several types of electronic levels that offer digital readouts instead of using a bubble gauge.

Most carpenter's levels contain three gauges: one for checking level (horizontal orientation), one for plumb (vertical orientation), and one for 45° angles. Some levels include pairs of gauges with opposing curves to improve readability.

Laser levels project highly accurate beams of light around rooms or along walls. Many styles automatically establish their own level orientation.

You should own at least two levels: a 2-foot carpenter's level for checking studs, joists, and other long construction surfaces, and a 8 to 9" torpedo level that is easy to carry in a tool belt and is perfect for checking shelves and other small workpieces. A 4-ft. version of the carpenter's level is most useful for framing projects.

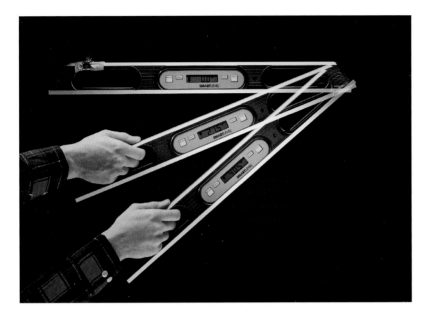

Battery-powered digital levels represent the latest advance in level design. Digital levels provide very accurate digital readouts, so you don't have to trust your eye when judging bubble position within a vial. Digital levels also measure slope and offer rise/run ratios, which are useful when building stairs. The electronic components are contained in a module that can be used alone as a torpedo level or inserted into frames of varying lengths.

Laser levels project a beam of light to create a level line all around a room or for level lines of longer lengths. A laser can eliminate the need for snapping chalk reference lines.

Make sure your level is accurate. Hold one side of the level against a flat, even surface (top photo), mark the location, and read the bubble gauge carefully. Pivot the level 180° (bottom photo) and read the gauge again. Next, flip the level over and read the gauge. The bubble should give the same reading each time. If not, adjust the mounting screws to calibrate the bubble, or buy a new level.

SQUARES

Squares come in many shapes and sizes, but they are all designed with one general purpose: to help you mark lumber and sheet goods for cutting.

A drywall T-square is large—it has a 4-foot arm so that you can make or mark straight cuts across a sheet of drywall or other sheet goods. A try square is great for marking crosscuts on 2 × 4s, but it is fixed, not adjustable like a combination square. A rafter square (also speed square) or a framing square is best for marking angles on rafters. Using the right tool will make your work more efficient and improve the accuracy of your cuts.

Familiarize yourself with the different types of squares and their uses so you can choose the right tool for the job.

Tip

If you are only going to buy one square, buy a large 10" or 12" polyethylene rafter square. They are inexpensive and very handy for marking and making crosscuts, the most common carpentry cuts you will make.

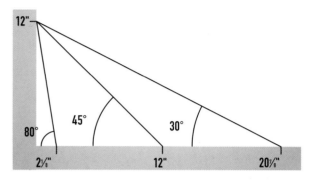

A framing square is commonly used to mark right angles on sheet goods and other large surfaces, but it can also be used to establish other angles by using different measurements along the body (long arm) and the tongue (short arm). The tool has gradations marked in tiny increments, and many come with detailed tables to help you make angles.

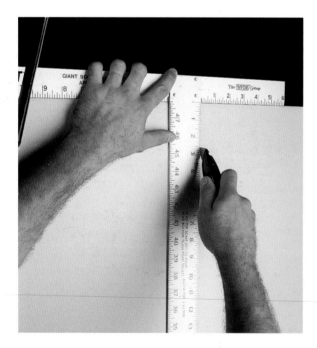

A drywall T-square simplifies the task of marking and cutting straight lines on sheets of drywall. The top of the T hooks over the edge of the drywall, while the leg is used as a straightedge. A T-square is also handy for marking cutting lines on plywood and other sheet goods. Some models have an adjustable T that can be set to common angles.

Common Framing Square Angles

Angle	Tongue	Body
30°	12"	20⅞"
45°	12"	12"
60°	12"	61⁵⁄₁₆"
70°	12"	4⅜"
75°	12"	3⁷⁄₃₂"
80°	12"	2⅛"

The chart above shows the markings to use on the framing square to obtain commonly required angles. If you want to make a line at a 30° angle, mark the workpiece at 12" on the tongue and 20⅞" on the body, and connect the marks with a straight line.

USING A COMBINATION SQUARE

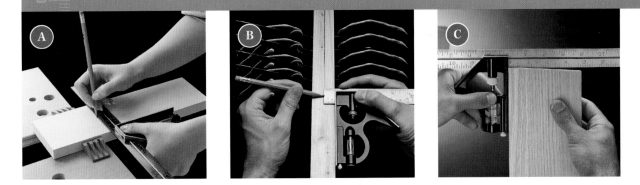

A   To mark a board for crosscutting, hold the square against the edge of the workpiece with the head locked, then use the edge of the blade to guide your pencil. Use the handle's 45° edge to mark boards for miter cuts.

B   To mark a line parallel to the edge of a board, lock the blade at the desired measurement, then hold the tip of the pencil along the end of the blade as you slide the tool along the workpiece. This is useful when marking reveal lines on window and door

C   To check for square, set the blade of a square flush with the end of the workpiece (and set the head flush with one edge). If the end is a true 90°, there will not be a gap between the blade and the workpiece.

USING A RAFTER SQUARE

A   To mark angle cuts, position the rafter square's pivot point against the edge of the workpiece, and set the tool so the desired angle marking is aligned with the same edge. Scribe a line to mark the angle on the workpiece. Flip the tool over to mark angles in the opposite direction.

B   To mark crosscuts, place a rafter square's raised edge flush with one edge of the board, and use the perpendicular edge to guide your pencil. On wide boards, you'll need to flip the square to the board's other edge to extend the line across the board.

C   To guide a circular saw when making crosscuts, first align the blade of the saw with your cutting line. As you cut, hold the raised edge of the square against the front edge of the workpiece and the perpendicular edge flush with the foot of the saw.

HANDSAWS

It's possible that you could do almost all your carpentry projects using a circular saw, power miter saw, or jigsaw and never miss a handsaw. However, there are times when using a handsaw is easier, more convenient, and produces better results. Handsaws also provide the do-it-yourselfer a cost-effective alternative to the higher price of power tools.

For every power saw available today, there is a handsaw available that was originally used to make the same type of cut.

There are many differences between handsaws. When you shop for a saw, look for one that's designed for the type of cutting you plan to do. Differences in handle design and the number, shape, and angle (set) of the teeth make each saw work best for specific applications.

For general carpentry cuts, use a crosscut saw with 8 to 10 teeth per inch. Crosscut saws have pointed teeth designed to slice through wood on the forward stroke and to deepen the cut and remove sawdust from the kerf on the back stroke.

Always use a handsaw for its intended purpose. Misuse of a handsaw will only damage the tool, dull the blade, or lead to injury.

When saw blades become dull, take them to a professional blade sharpener for tuning. It's worth the extra cost to ensure the job is done right.

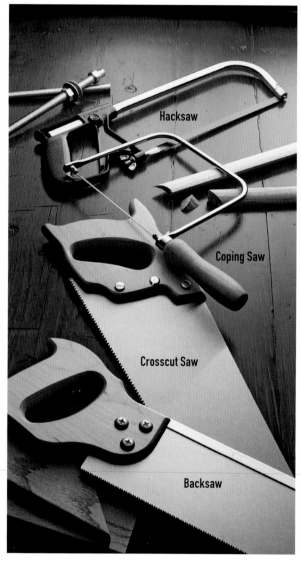

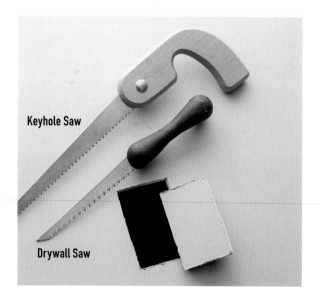

Making a cutout by hand requires a saw with a narrow, tapered blade that fits into confined spaces. Use a keyhole saw for making cutouts in plywood, paneling, and other thin materials and a drywall saw for making fixture cutouts in drywall.

Handsaws are less important today than they were a couple of generations ago. But keeping a few at hand is a good idea. A basic set includes a hacksaw, a coping saw, and a crosscut saw (preferably one that fits in your toolbox). A backsaw and miter box will expand your skills.

CHOOSING THE RIGHT HANDSAW

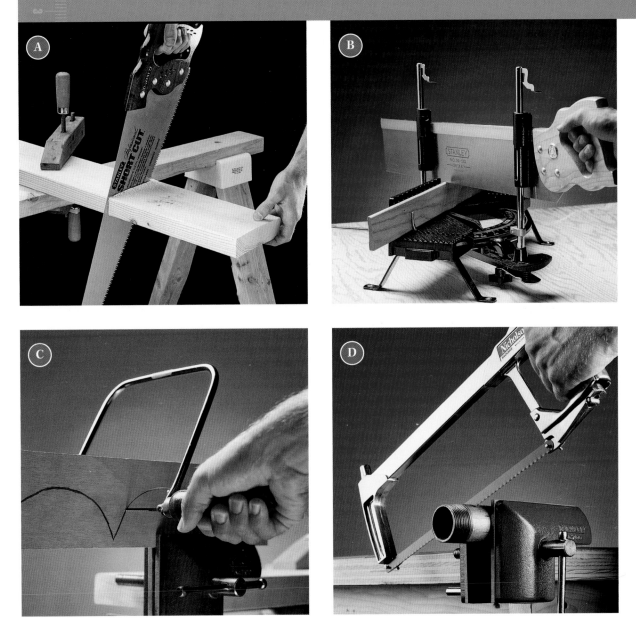

A   A crosscut saw comes in handy for single-cut projects or in confined spaces where power tools won't fit. At the end of a cut, saw slowly, and support waste material with your free hand to prevent splintering.

B   A backsaw with a miter box cuts precise angles on moldings and other trim. Clamp or hold the workpiece in the miter box and make sure the miter box is securely fastened to the work surface.

C   A coping saw has a thin, flexible blade designed to cut curves. It is also essential for making professional-looking joints in trim moldings. The blade of a coping saw breaks easily when under heavy use, so have extra blades on hand.

D   A hacksaw has a flexible, fine-tooth blade designed to cut metal. Carpenters use hacksaws to cut plumbing pipe or to cut away stubborn metal fasteners. To avoid breaking the blade, make sure the blade is stretched tightly in the frame before cutting.

HAMMERS

The standard hammer is a 16-ounce, curved-claw finish hammer. It is designed for driving, setting, and pulling nails. Choose a hammer with a smooth finish, a high-carbon steel head, and a quality handle made of hickory, fiberglass, or solid steel. Less expensive steel handles often have hollow cores that are not as efficient at transmitting force to the head. This is a tool that needs to feel comfortable, so heft all the finish hammers available before purchasing.

Straight-claw framing hammers—usually with a 20-ounce or heavier head—are used for framing walls and other heavy-duty tasks. The extra weight helps drive large nails with fewer swings. Most framing hammers are too heavy for finish carpentry, where control is of primary importance.

A mallet with a non-marking rubber or plastic head is the best tool for driving chisels without damaging the tools. Mallets are also useful for making slight adjustments to a workpiece without marring the surface of the wood.

A sledgehammer or maul is effective for demolishing old construction or adjusting the position of framing members.

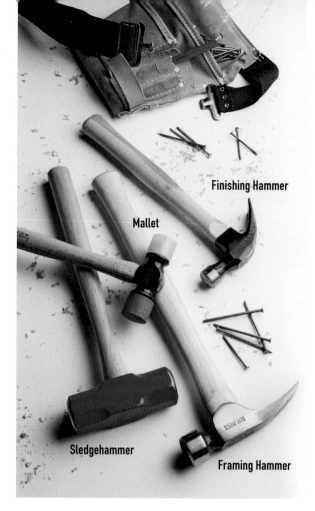

A hammer is not a one-size-fits-all tool. For most homeowners, a finishing hammer with a claw will be the hammer most often used, but it's beneficial to have on hand a mallet, sledgehammer, and large framing hammer if you will be tackling large carpentry projects.

Framing hammers vary in size, length, and handle material. Handle types include fiberglass, solid steel, hollow core, and wood. Hammers typically range in length from 14 to 18". Most framing hammers have a head weighing at least 20 oz., but lighter and heavier models are available. Some heads feature a waffle pattern across the face that increases the hammer's hold on the nail for more efficiency and accuracy. Framing hammers have straight claws for prying boards.

Skillbuilder

Buy a box of 2" common or box nails. Grab some scrap 2× lumber (construction sites have lots of these) and facenail the pieces together. Drive lots and lots of nails, from both sides. Drive the nails with the lumber on a solid surface (cement floor). Drive the nails with the lumber on a springy surface (upholstered furniture). Notice a difference? Use the nail-encrusted boards as a doorstop.

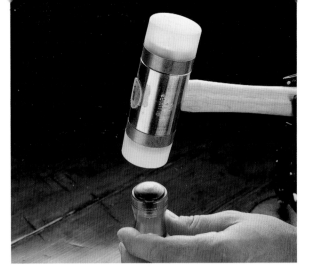

Use a sledgehammer to demolish wall framing and to drive spikes and stakes. Sledgehammers vary in weight from 2 to 20 lbs., and in length from 10 to 36".

A mallet with a rubber or plastic head drives woodworking chisels. A soft mallet will not damage fine woodworking tools.

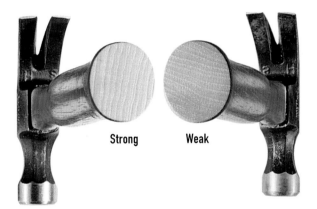

Strong   Weak

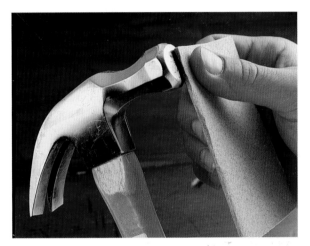

The strongest wooden tool handles have wood grain that runs parallel to the tool head (left). Handles with the grain running perpendicular to the tool head (right) are more likely to break. Check the end grain before buying a new tool or tool handle. Tool handles that are cracked or loose should be replaced. Wood handles absorb more shock than fiberglass or metal.

A new hammer may have a very smooth face that tends to slip off the heads of nails. Rough up the face with sandpaper to increase friction between the hammer and the nail. You can also use fine sandpaper to remove wood resins and nail coatings that build up on the face of your hammers. For finish hammering, you may want to stick with a smooth-face hammer.

Pulling Nails with a Hammer

To pull nails with a claw hammer, place a block of wood under the hammer head for added leverage and to avoid damage to the workpiece. If you are pulling large nails or many nails, use a pry bar or cat's paw.

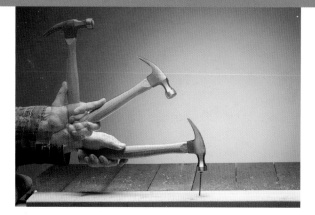

Hold the hammer with a relaxed grip: Take advantage of the hammer's momentum and weight by releasing your wrist at the bottom of the swing as if you were throwing the head of the hammer onto the nail. Hit the nail squarely on the head, repeating the motion until the nail head is flush with the work surface.

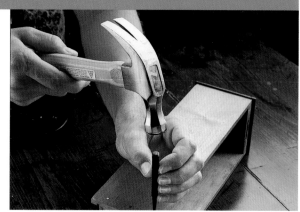

To set a finish nail below the surface, position the tip of a nail set on the nail head and strike the other end with a hammer.

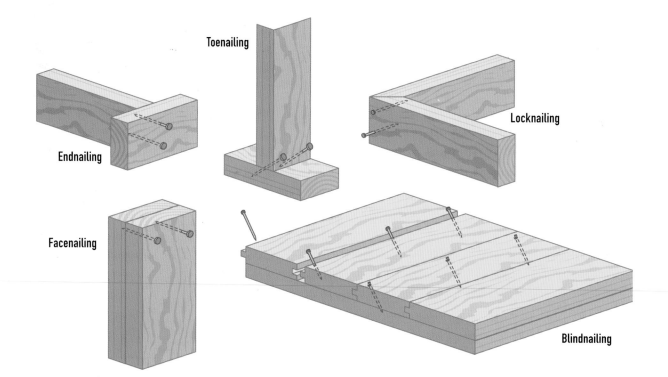

Use the proper nailing technique for the task. Endnailing is used to attach perpendicular boards when moderate strength is required. Toenail at a 45° angle for extra strength when joining perpendicular framing members. Facenail to create strong headers for door and window openings. Blindnail tongue-and-groove boards to conceal nails, eliminating the need to set nails and cover them with putty before painting or staining. Locknail outside miter joints in both directions on trim projects to prevent gaps from developing as the trim pieces dry.

Use a screwdriver or screw bit that closely matches the screw head. A tip that's too big or too small will damage the screw and the driver, and it will make the screw hard to remove later. This screwdriver is too small for the screw—the blades should fit all the way into the screw head.

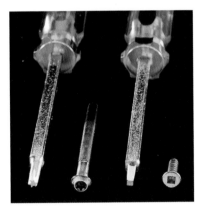

Other driving options include square-drive and Torx-drive screws. Square-drive screwdrivers are gaining popularity because square-drive screws are difficult to strip. Torx-drivers are used on electronics, tools, and automotive applications.

SCREWDRIVERS

Every carpenter should own several Phillips and slotted screwdrivers. Even though the drill-mounted screw bit has become the standard for large projects, screwdrivers are still essential for a variety of carpentry tasks. Look for quality screwdrivers with hardened-steel blades and handles that are easy to grip. Other features to look for include insulated handles to protect against electrical shock and oxide-coated tips for a strong hold on screw heads. For working in tight spots, a screwdriver with a magnetic head can also be helpful.

Cordless power screwdrivers save time and effort. For small projects, they are an inexpensive alternative to a cordless drill or screw gun. Most models include a removable battery pack and charger, so you can keep one battery in the charger at all times. Cordless power screwdrivers have a universal ¼" drive and come with a slotted bit and a #2 Phillips bit. Other bits, such as Torx and socket bits are also available.

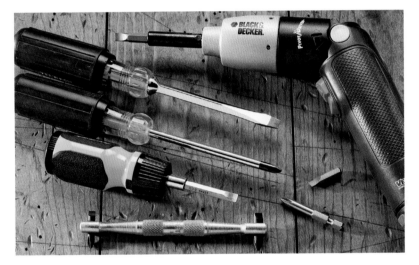

Common screwdrivers include: slot screwdriver with insulated handle, Phillips screwdriver with insulated handle and oxide tip for better control, spiral ratchet driver with interchangeable bits, offset screwdriver for driving in tight places, and cordless power screwdriver with battery pack and pivoting shaft.

Skillbuilder

Using #8 by 1¼" Phillips head wood screws and a scrap of 2× lumber, drive a screw (by hand) without drilling a pilot hole. Then drill 1/16", 3/32", 1/8", 5/32", and 3/16" pilot holes. Drive a screw into each hole. Notice that it is difficult to drive the screw so that it is flush with the wood surface. That's because wood screws have a shank and a straight taper. Drill a 5/32" to a depth to match the screw shank.

Then extend that hole with a 1/16" bit. This is called countersinking. Drive a screw into this hole and it is easier to make the head flush. Special countersink-pilot hole drill bits are available to repeat this process as one step. Bugle head screws countersink themselves, as they have no shank and a fluted head. See page 55 Common Drill Bits for more information on drilling.

CLAMPS & VISES

Vises and clamps are used to hold workpieces in place during cutting or other tasks and to hold pieces together while glue sets.

Your workbench should include a heavy-duty carpenter's vise. For specialty clamping jobs, a wide variety of clamps are available, including C-clamps, locking pliers, handscrews, web clamps, or ratchet-type clamps.

For clamping wide stock, use pipe clamps or bar clamps. The jaws of pipe clamps are connected by a steel pipe. The distance between the jaws is limited only by the length of the pipe.

Use handscrews to hold materials together at various angles while glue is drying. Handscrews are wooden clamps with two adjusting screws. The jaws won't damage wood surfaces.

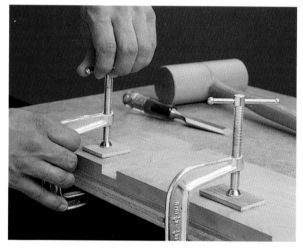

Use C-clamps for clamping jobs from 1 to 6". To protect workpieces, place scrap wood blocks between the jaws of the clamp and the workpiece surface.

Use ratchet-type clamps to clamp a workpiece quickly and easily. Large ratchet-type clamps can span up to 4 ft. and can be tightened with one hand while supporting the workpiece with the other hand.

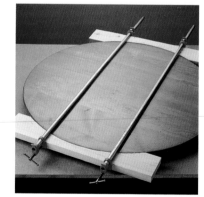

Hold large workpieces with pipe clamps or bar clamps. Bar clamps are sold with the bars. Pipe clamp jaws are available to fit ½" or ¾" diameter pipe of any length.

Mount a sturdy bench vise on the end of your workbench to hold workpieces securely. Select a vise that adjusts easily and has a minimum jaw opening of about 4".

CHISELS

A wood chisel consists of a sharp steel blade beveled on one face and set in a wood or plastic handle. It cuts with light hand pressure or when the end of the handle is tapped with a mallet. A wood chisel is often used to cut hinge and lock mortises.

When creating deep cuts, make several shallow cuts instead of one deep cut. Forcing a chisel to make deep cuts only dulls the tool and can damage the workpiece.

Sharpen the blades of your chisels often (see following pages). Chisels are easier and safer to use and produce better results when they are sharp.

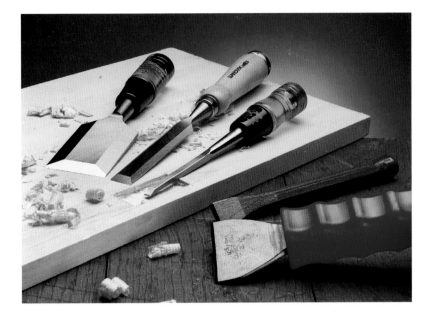

Types of chisels include (from left to right): a framing chisel, used for rough trimming of lumber; a mortise chisel, for framing hinge and lock mortises; a small wood chisel, for light-duty wood carving; cold chisel that is made of solid steel and is used for cutting through metal; and a mason's chisel, for cutting stone and masonry.

CHISELING A MORTISE

1   Cut the outline of the mortise. Hold the chisel bevel-side-in and tap the butt end lightly with a mallet until the cut has reached the proper depth.

2   Make a series of parallel depth cuts ¼" apart across the mortise, with the chisel held at a 45° angle. Drive the chisel with light mallet blows to the handle.

3   Pry out waste chips by holding the chisel at a low angle with the beveled side toward the work surface. Drive the chisel using light hand pressure.

SHARPENING CHISELS & PLANE BLADES

It is a good idea to sharpen chisels and plane blades before each use, even if the tools are brand new. The factory edges on new blades are sharpened by machine and are not as sharp as hand-sharpened blades.

Sharpening a tool blade is a two-step process. First, the tool is rough-ground on an electric bench grinder, then it is finish-honed on a fine-grit sharpening stone. If you do not have a bench grinder, you can use a coarse-grit sharpening stone to rough-grind the blade.

Tools & Materials

Bench grinder or coarse-grit sharpening stone
Work gloves

Fine-grit sharpening stone
Cup of water
Light machine oil

Tip: Sponge Bath

One way to keep the blade cool when grinding is to hot-glue a piece of sponge to the back of the blade near the cutting edge. Dip the blade in water. The sponge holds water against the back of the blade to draw off heat. When the sponge gets warm, wet it again.

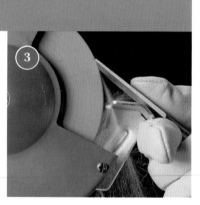

SHARPENING CHISELS & PLANE BLADES ON A GRINDER

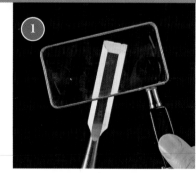

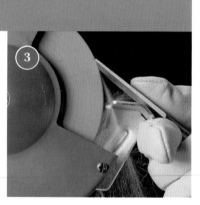

1   Inspect the cutting edge for nicks. Before the blade can be honed on a sharpening stone, any nicks in the steel must be completely removed by grinding.

2   Grind off nicks, using a bench grinder with a medium-grit wheel. Hold the tool on the flat portion of the tool rest, with the beveled side facing up. Hold the tip against the wheel and move it from side to side. Make sure the cutting edge remains square, and cool the blade frequently in water.

3   Rough-grind the cutting edge by turning the blade so that the beveled side is down. Rest the blade on the angled portion of the tool rest. Move the blade from side to side against the wheel to grind the tip to a 20° bevel, checking often with an angle gauge. Cool the metal frequently in water while grinding.

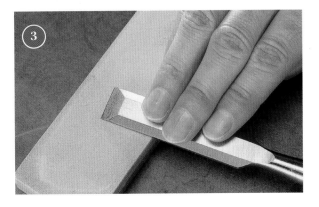

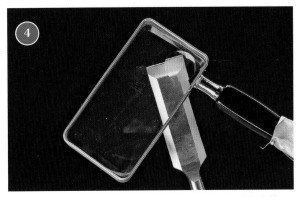

1   Finish-hone the cutting edge on a fine-grit sharpening stone. Place a few drops of light machine oil on the stone to lubricate the steel and to float away grit and filings. Hold the blade at a 25° angle so the bevel is flat against the stone. Draw it several times across the stone, lifting it away after each pass. Wipe the stone often with a clean rag, and apply oil after each wiping.

2   Put a "micro-bevel" on the blade by lifting it slightly so only the tip touches the stone. Draw the blade two or three times across the stone, until a slight burr can be felt along the back of the blade.

3   Turn the blade over. Holding the blade flat, draw it across the stone one or two times to remove the burr.

4   Examine the cutting edge of the blade. The fine micro-bevel should be about 1/16" wide. The micro-bevel gives the chisel its razor-sharp edge.

Tip: Keep Your Temper

Keep a container of cool water close by when grinding a tool blade. Dip the blade in water frequently to prevent heat from ruining the temper of the steel. When the beads of water on the blade evaporate, it should be dipped again.

PLANES &
SURFACE-FORMING RASPS

Common carpentry planes include: a jack plane, for trimming framing lumber, doors, and other large workpieces; a power planer, for removing lots of material quickly; a block plane, for shaving material from trim and other narrow workpieces; and surface-forming rasps, for trimming flat or curved surfaces.

Planes are designed for removing shavings of material from lumber when a saw would cut off too much material and sanding would remove too little. A hand plane consists of a razor-sharp cutting blade, or iron, set in a steel or wood base. Adjusting the blade requires some trial and error. After making an adjustment, test the plane on a scrap piece before using it on your workpiece. Usually, the shallower the blade is set, the better the plane cuts.

The blade on a surface-forming rasp can't be adjusted, but interchangeable blades are available for fine and rough work. Surface-forming rasp blades have a series of holes stamped in the metal, so shavings seldom become clogged in the tool's blade.

If you plan on planing many large workpieces, consider purchasing a power planer. A power planer does the job more quickly than a hand plane and with equally fine results.

Use a block plane for common jobs, like trimming end grain, planing the edges of particleboard and plywood, and trimming laminates.

Skillbuilder

Buy a short 1 × 4 pine board, poplar board, and maple or oak board. (Yes, expensive!). Clamp the pine into a vise. Operate the plane so the wood grain runs "uphill" ahead of the plane. Grip the toe knob and handle firmly, and plane with long, smooth strokes. To prevent overplaning at the beginning and end of the board, called dipping, press down on the toe knob at the beginning of the stroke and bear down on the heel at the end of the stroke. Try planing the other direction. Repeat with the other two boards. Try planing on the face of the board—you will need to secure it below the surface of the wood so it doesn't move and the plane can move freely.

To change power planer blades, remove the screws and gib bars that hold the blades in place and carefully remove the dull blade. Wear gloves to protect your hands. For double-edged blades, flip the blade to the fresh edge and reinstall. Tighten the gib screws securely.

Turn the planer's cutting depth dial to set the amount of material you'll remove with each pass. Limit cutting depth to ⅛" or less to prevent overloading the motor and to ensure a smooth cut.

Draw layout lines on your workpiece to mark the amount of material you need to plane away. Make repeated passes with the planer until it reaches the layout lines. Keep an eye on your layout lines as you work to make sure the planer removes material evenly.

Power Planer Overview

Traditional hand planes are still used by both carpenters and woodworkers, but it takes practice to sharpen, adjust, and use them properly. If you're not experienced with hand planes, a power planer may be a better choice for your carpentry projects. It's much easier to set up and operate, and it will generally plane away material more quickly than a hand plane.

Typical power planers have two narrow blades mounted in a cylindrical-shaped cutterhead. The cutterhead spins at high speeds to provide the planing action. Power planer blades are made of carbide, which stays sharp much longer than a conventional steel plane blade. When the blades dull, they do not need to be resharpened. Instead, you simply remove them from the cutterhead and replace. Most power planers have double-edged blades, so you have a second sharp edge to use before it's necessary to buy new blades.

To use a power planer, set the depth of cut by turning a dial on the front of the tool. This raises the front portion of the planer's sole to expose the cutters. Limit your cutting depth to not more than ⅛" on softwood and 1/16" on hardwoods like oak or maple. If possible, connect the planer to a dust bag or shop vacuum to collect the planer shavings; these tools make considerable debris quickly. Start the planer and slide it slowly along the wood to make the cut, keeping the sole of the tool pressed firmly against the workpiece. Push down on the front of the planer as you begin the cut, then transfer pressure to the rear of the planer as you reach the end of the cut. If you are planing both across the grain and along it, make the cross-grain passes first, then finish up with long-grain passes. This will allow you to plane away any tearout or chipping that occurs on the cross-grain passes.

As you make each pass, apply more hand pressure on the front of the tool to begin, then transfer pressure to the rear as you end the cut. Slide the tool smoothly and slowly so the motor doesn't labor in the cut.

JIGSAWS

The jigsaw is a very good portable power tool for cutting curves and internal cutouts. The cutting capacity of a jigsaw depends on its power and the length of its blade stroke. Choose a saw rated to cut 2-inch-thick softwood and ¾-inch-thick hardwood stock. Many jigsaws have a pivoting baseplate that can be locked so you can make bevel cuts as well.

A variable-speed jigsaw is the best choice, because different blade styles require different cutting speeds for best results. In general, faster blade speeds are used for cutting with coarse-tooth blades and slower speeds with fine-tooth blades.

Jigsaws vibrate more than other power saws because of the up-and-down blade action. However, top-quality jigsaws have a heavy-gauge steel baseplate that reduces vibration to help you hold the saw tightly against the workpiece for better control.

Because jigsaw blades cut on the upward stroke, the top side of the workpiece may splinter. If the wood has a good side to protect, cut with this surface facing downward.

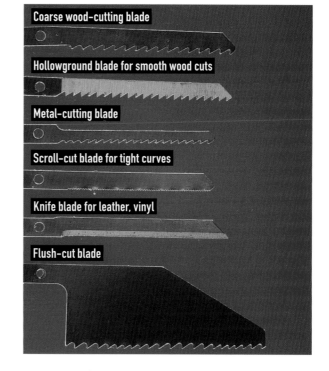

Coarse wood-cutting blade

Hollowground blade for smooth wood cuts

Metal-cutting blade

Scroll-cut blade for tight curves

Knife blade for leather, vinyl

Flush-cut blade

Jigsaw blades come in an array of designs for cutting different materials. Choose the right blade for the job. With fine-tooth blades that have 14 or more teeth per inch, set the saw at a low speed. Coarse blades require faster blade speeds.

Do not force blades. Jigsaw blades are flexible and may bend or break if forced. Move the saw slowly when cutting bevels or tough material like knots in wood.

Skillbuilder

Buy a 2 × 4 ft. ½" piece of plywood. Use a compass or various round shapes to trace circles on the board ranging from 2" to 10". Drill a ¼" hole along the inside edge of the line, but not crossing to the outside. Insert the jigsaw into the hole and cut out the circle. Cut out a circle with the workpiece clamped to a solid surface. Cut out another circle without clamping. When you have cut out all the holes, add legs to your holey board and use it as a bean bag toss game!

Make plunge cuts by tipping the saw so the front edge of the baseplate is held firmly against the workpiece. Start the saw, and slowly lower it to a horizontal position, letting the blade gradually cut through the workpiece.

Cut metals with a fine-tooth metal-cutting blade and select a slow blade speed. Support sheet metals with thin plywood to eliminate vibration. Use emery paper or a file to smooth burred edges left by the blade.

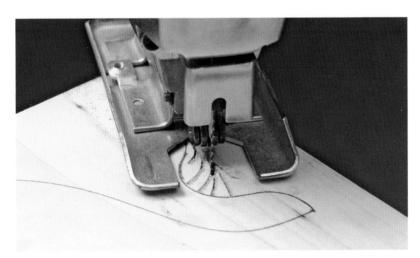

The jigsaw is designed to cut curves, but tight curves can cause the blade to bind. An easy way to avoid this problem is to make a series of relief cuts through the surrounding waste material and up to the curved cutting line. This way you can break up a tight curve into smaller sections rather than one long cut.

Tip

To get the best possible cut with a jigsaw, clamp your workpiece securely to a solid work station. Even though the saw is meant to be held with one hand, it usually works better to use both hands for guidance. And remember, don't force it!

CIRCULAR SAWS

A portable circular saw has become the most frequently used cutting tool for do-it-yourselfers. With the right set of blades, you can use a circular saw to cut wood, metal, plaster, concrete, or other masonry materials. An adjustable baseplate lets you set the blade depth for your workpiece, and it also pivots from side to side for bevel cuts.

Most professional carpenters use a 7¼-inch-blade circular saw. For home carpentry, 7¼-inch-blade and 6½-inch-blade models are the most popular. A smaller blade means a smaller, lighter saw body, but bear in mind that a smaller saw is usually less powerful and is limited when cutting bevel cuts or material that is thicker than 2× stock.

Cordless circular saws have 5⅜-inch-wide blades—wide enough to cut through sheet goods or to make square cuts on 2× lumber. Cordless models are useful in situations where a power cord gets in the way. However, most cordless circular saws aren't powerful enough to be the primary cutting tool for big projects.

Because circular saw blades cut in an upward direction, the top face of the workpiece may splinter. To protect the finished side of the workpiece, mark measurements on the back side and place the good side down for cutting.

Get the most out of your saw by inspecting your blade regularly and changing it as needed (page 34). You can also improve your results with a straightedge guide (page 38), which makes it easier to cut long stock precisely.

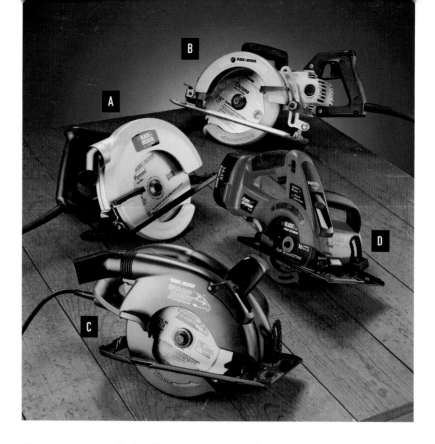

Common types of circular saws include: (A) 7¼"-blade, standard-drive saw. Standard-drive circular saws are the most popular choice among do-it-yourselfers and are widely used by professional carpenters. This model has a sawdust-release pipe that connects to a collection bag. (B) 7¼"-blade, worm-drive saw. Some carpenters prefer the worm-drive saw for heavy-duty cutting. Worm-drive saws offer more torque at any given speed. As a result, they are less likely to slow, bind, or kick back when subjected to a heavy load. (C) 6½"-blade, standard-drive saw. Do-it-yourselfers looking for a lightweight saw may want to consider a standard-drive saw with a 6½" blade. This model has a convenient window for an easy view of the line while cutting. (D) 5⅜"-blade, cordless trim saw. Cordless trim saws are convenient for cutting trim and other thin stock, especially when the work site is outdoors or away from an electrical receptacle.

Tip

Using your circular saw to cut masonry is possible, but probably not the best idea. If you need to cut masonry (pavers, concrete, stone) rent a dedicated masonry wet saw. A wet saw uses a small stream of water to make the cutting easier and keep down the dust. A masonry saw has the power to handle this tough material.

Circular Saw Blade Options

To get full use from your circular saw, you'll need an assortment of blades designed for specific cutting tasks. Your collection should include at least one general-purpose combination blade with carbide teeth. In addition to cutting wood and sheet material, you can also use a circular saw to cut masonry and thin metal with the appropriate abrasive blade. Here are the main types of circular saw blades:

- Remodeling blade: Designed to make both ripcuts and crosscuts in construction lumber that may also be embedded with nails or screws. It will have a low tooth count and tall shoulders behind the teeth to prevent them from cutting too aggressively or breaking on metal. It's a good choice for opening wall cavities or removing exterior or floor sheathing.
- Ripping/general framing blade: Higher tooth counts than a remodeling blade, usually ranging from 16 to 24 teeth. A suitable blade for fast rip cuts in construction plywood and general crosscuts in framing lumber. Fewer teeth will produce more splintering, so this is not a blade for finish cutting.
- General-purpose blade: The workhorse blade of most circular saws, these blades will have 30 to 40 teeth and are good choices for fast, semi-smooth wood cutting in any direction.
- Fine crosscutting blade: A 40- to 60-tooth blade designed to make smooth crosscuts in veneered plywood with minimal splintering.
- Masonry or metal-cutting blade: A toothless blade made of special abrasives for cutting cinder block, concrete, and both ferrous and non-ferrous metal. Be sure to wear a dust mask when using these blades; abrasive particles and masonry dust are hazardous to breathe.

Skillbuilder

Use a combination or rafter square to mark 45° miters across the faces of four 2 × 4 or 2 × 6 pieces of lumber to make four equal-length pieces. The miters need to be opposing, not parallel. Make the miter cuts. Glue, clamp, and locknail or screw the pieces together to make a square. You've made a heavy duty picture frame! Repeat the process, except this time set the saw blade at 45° and bevel across the ends of the boards. Assemble these pieces into a square. If your measuring and cutting were accurate, your squares should actually be square. For future reference, miter usually means cutting an angle across the face (broad side) of a piece, and bevel means shaving or cutting along an edge or end of a board.

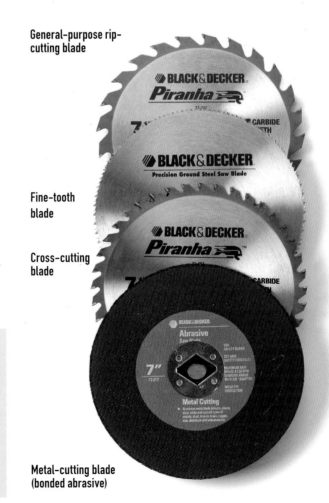

General-purpose rip-cutting blade

Fine-tooth blade

Cross-cutting blade

Metal-cutting blade (bonded abrasive)

SETTING THE BLADE DEPTH

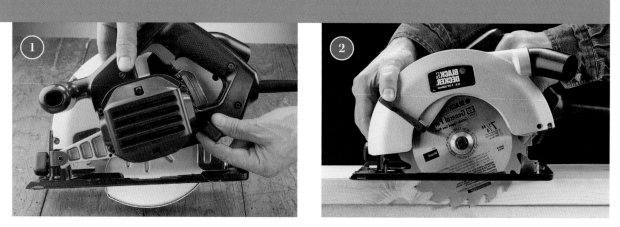

1   The blade on a circular saw does not move when you set the blade depth. Instead, on most circular saws, the saw baseplate pivots up and down, changing the amount of blade that is exposed. Unplug the saw, then pull out the depth adjustment lever and slide it up or down to adjust the blade depth.

2   Pull up on the blade guard lever to expose the blade, then position the blade flush with the edge of the workpiece to check the setting. The blade should extend beyond the bottom of the workpiece by no more than the depth of a saw tooth. Release the knob to lock the blade. Note: Some saws have a baseplate that drops rather than pivots. When the knob is pulled out, the entire baseplate can be moved up or down.

CHANGING A CIRCULAR SAW BLADE

1   Unplug the saw and inspect the blade, wearing gloves to protect your hands. Replace the blade if you find worn, cracked, or chipped teeth. Remove the blade for cleaning if sticky resin or pitch has accumulated.

2   To loosen the blade, first depress the arbor lock button or lever to lock the blade in position, then loosen the bolt with a wrench and slide the bolt and washer out of the assembly. On older models with no arbor lock, insert a wood block between the blade and baseplate to keep the blade from turning as you loosen the bolt.

3   Install a new blade. Or, if the old blade is soiled but in otherwise good condition, clean and reinstall it. Use the directional markings on the side of the blade as a guide when attaching a blade. Insert the bolt and washer, then tighten the bolt with a wrench until the bolt is snug. Do not overtighten.

MAKING CROSSCUTS

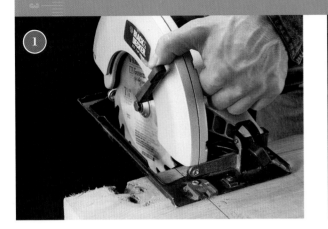
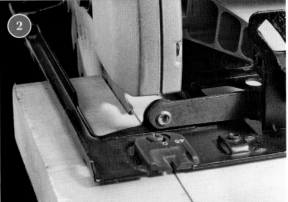

1   Secure the workpiece with clamps and position the baseplate with the blade approximately 1" from the edge. Align the guide mark with the cutting line. The saw will remove a small amount of material on each side of the blade. If your project requires exact cuts, make your first cut in the waste area. You can make a second pass with the saw, as necessary, to remove more material.

2   While holding the saw with two hands, squeeze the trigger and guide the blade into the workpiece, following the cutting line with the guide mark and applying steady pressure as you push the saw forward. The guide mark on every saw is different. If you will be cutting material with someone else's saw, make a few practice cuts to familiarize yourself with the new saw.

MAKING PLUNGE CUTS

1   Support the workpiece by clamping it down on sawhorses. Clamp a 2 × 4 on the edge as a guide. Retract the blade guard and position the saw so the front edge of the foot, not the blade, is against the workpiece.

2   Hold the saw with two hands as you make the cut. Start the saw, and slowly lower the blade into the workpiece, keeping the baseplate against the 2 × 4.

A   Attach a commercial straightedge guide to the baseplate of your circular saw. Generally, straight-cutting guides that mount to the saw are accurate enough but they are not precise. For maximum precision, try clamping cutting guides to your work surface.

B   It's much safer to cut up full-sized, heavy sheets of plywood with a circular saw than a table saw. Lay the sheet over several pieces of framing lumber to provide room for the blade underneath. Set the blade depth so the teeth protrude about ¼" below the plywood. Once the sheets are cut into manageable sizes, you can make finish cuts on the table saw. Clamp a straightedge guide to the workpiece.

Tips for Circular Saw Success

Circular saws are powerful, heavy, and potentially dangerous. To get the best possible results, take the time to use the saw correctly. Use a stable base to saw on, and clamp the workpiece down so it does not move. Do not hold a piece of wood against your thigh and saw off the end! Not only are you endangering your limbs, you will not get a quality cut.

Maintaining a steady travel speed is important. When making long rip cuts, make sure both sides of the material are supported so the blade does not get pinched. Make sure you have the room to maneuver during the cut, and that the cord is long enough to make the cut.

Finally, circular saws are noisy dust makers--protect your eyes, nose, and ears.

MAKING BEVEL CUTS

Tip

Copy existing angles with a T-bevel. Transpose the cutting line to your workpiece and adjust the angle of your circular saw to cut on the line.

1   Loosen the bevel adjustment knob and slide the knob to the required setting. Some models have a setscrew for common angles such as 90° (no bevel) and 45°. Tighten the knob.

2   Position the baseplate of your saw on the workpiece. As you cut, sight down the blade to ensure it remains aligned with the cutting line on the waste side of the workpiece.

CUTTING DADOES

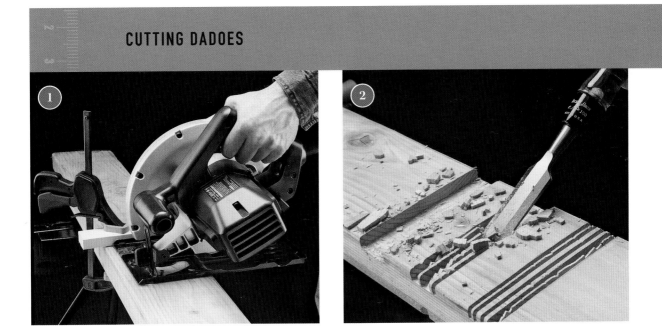

1   To cut dadoes with a circular saw, set the blade depth to ⅓ the desired depth of the dado, and mark the outside edges where you want the dado. Secure the workpiece with a clamp and cut the outside lines using a straightedge. Make several parallel passes between the outside cuts, every ¼".

2   Clean out the material between the kerfs with a wood chisel. To avoid gouging the workpiece, apply hand pressure or tap the chisel with the bevel side up using a mallet. For more information on chisels, see page 25.

STRAIGHTEDGE GUIDES

Making straight and accurate rip cuts or cutting long sheets of plywood or paneling is a challenge. Even the best carpenter can't always keep the blade on the cutline, especially over a longer span. A straightedge guide or jig solves the problem. As long as you keep the saw's baseplate pressed against the cleat as you make the cut, you're assured of a straight cut on your workpiece.

For accurate cutting, the cleat must have a perfectly straight edge. Ask at the lumber yard if they will cut the cleat using their panel saw.

Tools & Materials

C-clamps
Pencil
Circular saw
¼" finish plywood base
  (12 × 96")

¾" plywood cleat
  (2 × 96")
Carpenter's glue

A straightedge guide overcomes the difficulty of making square rip cuts and other square cuts on long workpieces. The guide's flat edge ensures that any cuts made with it will be flat as well.

BUILDING A STRAIGHTEDGE GUIDE

1   Apply carpenter's glue to the bottom of the ¾" plywood cleat, then position the cleat on the ¼" plywood base, 3" from one edge. Clamp the pieces together until the glue dries.

2   Position the circular saw with its wide foot tight against the ¾" plywood cleat on the wide side of the plywood. Cut away the excess portion of the plywood base with a single pass of the saw to create a square, flat edge. Repeat on the other side with the narrow foot.

3   To use the guide, position it on top of the workpiece, so the guide's flat edge is flush with the cutting line on the workpiece. Clamp the guide in place with C-clamps. Typically you will only use the wide side, but at times you may need to use the narrow side.

POWER MITER SAWS

Power miter saws are versatile, portable tools that are used to cut angles in trim, framing lumber, and other narrow stock.

The blade assembly of a power miter saw swivels up to 45° in either direction, allowing it to make straight, mitered, and beveled cuts. However, when the assembly is turned to a 45° angle, the cutting depth is considerably shortened.

If you are considering buying or renting a power miter saw for a specific project, such as building a deck, don't assume that every saw will have the capacity to cut wider boards at a 45° angle. Ask the salesperson about the maximum cutting capacity for each saw at a 45° angle, and make sure the saw you choose can make clean cuts through the stock you use most frequently.

A compound miter saw (opposite page, top) has a second pivot point on the blade assembly that makes it possible to cut a bevel and miter angle at the same time. This option is useful when cutting cove moldings. See page 46, for more information about compound miter cuts.

The biggest limitation of a power miter saw is cutting extra-wide stock. A sliding compound miter saw (opposite page, bottom) eliminates this limitation. The entire blade assembly is mounted on a sliding carriage, giving the saw a much greater cutting capacity than a standard or compound miter saw. For tips on cutting extra-wide boards without a sliding compound miter saw, see page 44.

The power miter saw has evolved from a new and relatively rare tool just a generation ago into the workhorse tool found in most home workshops today. It combines speed, accuracy, and fast set-up time, and as it's become more popular, it's become quite affordable.

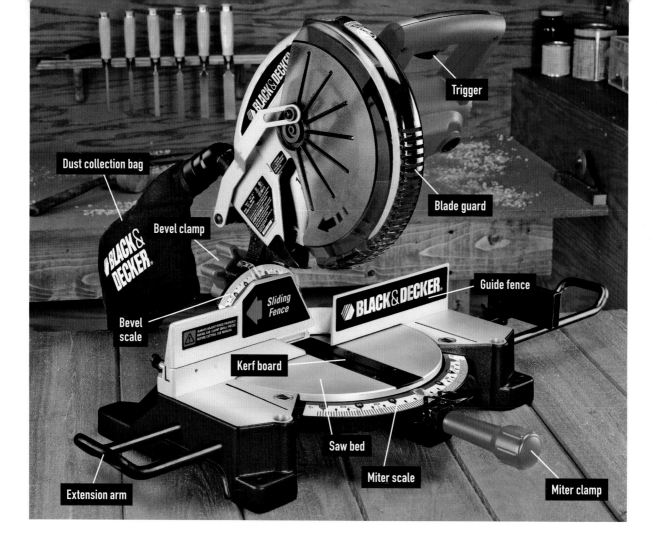

Trigger

Dust collection bag

Bevel clamp

Blade guard

BLACK & DECKER

Bevel scale

Sliding Fence

ALWAYS ADJUST FENCE PROPERLY BEFORE USE. CLAMP SMALL PIECES BEFORE CUTTING. SEE MANUAL.

Guide fence

Kerf board

Saw bed

Miter scale

Miter clamp

Extension arm

A compound miter saw cuts bevels and miters at the same time. The miter and bevel scales make it easy to set the saw quickly for precise angles. Before cutting, make sure the material is flush with the guide fence. Otherwise, the angle you cut will be incorrect. Extension arms provide a safe way to hold longer materials in place. Some models also offer stock clamps that secure workpieces to the saw table. Always remove debris or small wood scraps that may be blocking the kerf board before beginning any cut, and remember to empty the dust collection bag regularly.

Sliding carriage

A sliding compound miter saw has all the components of a regular compound miter saw, with the addition of a sliding blade assembly that makes it possible to cut much wider stock.

Skillbuilder

Repeat the Skillbuilder exercise from the circular saw section (page 33) using the miter saw instead.

Power Miter Saw Blades & Their Applications

The quality of the cut produced by a power miter saw depends on the blade you use and the speed at which the blade is forced through the workpiece. Let the motor reach full speed before cutting, then lower the blade assembly slowly for the best results.

A 16-tooth carbide-tipped blade cuts quickly and is good for rough-cutting framing lumber.

A 60-tooth carbide-tipped blade makes smooth cuts in both softwoods and hardwoods. It is a good all-purpose blade for general carpentry work.

CHANGING THE BLADE ON A POWER MITER SAW

1   Unplug the saw and inspect the blade; check for dull or damaged teeth.

2   If the blade is dull or is the wrong type for the material you want to cut, depress the arbor lock button and turn the arbor nut on the blade clockwise to remove it.

3   When the nut is free, carefully remove the blade and slide the new blade into position. Tighten the arbor nut until snug. Do not overtighten the nut.

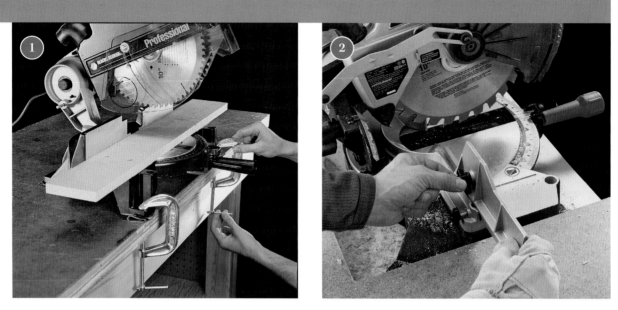

1   Anchor the saw to a stationary workbench, using C-clamps. To support long moldings or other stock, build a pair of blocks the height of the saw table, using 1× lumber. Align the blocks with the saw fence and clamp them to the workbench.

2   Position the adjustable fence to support the workpiece, then tighten the fence clamp.

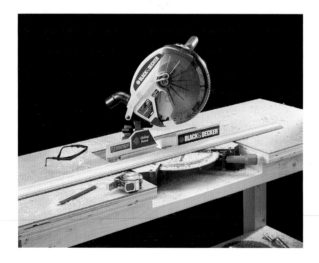

Option: Consider building a cutting table with a recessed area the same depth as the saw bed. The table will support longer stock, eliminating the need for support arms.

Option: Rent or buy a portable power miter saw table for extensive cutting of long stock. Or, use a portable workbench and a roller-type support stand to support your saw and workpieces.

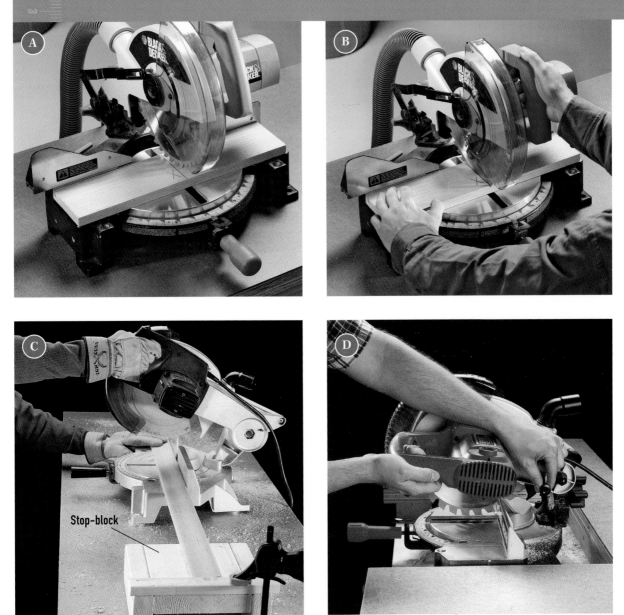

Stop-block

A   It's easy to make precise crosscuts on a miter saw with this simple procedure. First, lower the blade so the edges of the teeth meet your cutting line. Make sure the blade will cut on the waste side of the line.

B   Hold the workpiece securely against the saw table and fence, and raise the motor arm to its highest position. Start the saw and pivot the blade slowly into the wood to make the cut.

C   To cut multiple pieces of stock to the same length, clamp a stop block to your support table at the desired distance from the blade. After cutting the first piece, position each additional length against the stop block and the fence to cut pieces of equal length.

D   Lock the saw assembly in the down position when storing or moving it or when you won't be using it for a long period of time.

CUTTING EXTRA-WIDE BOARDS

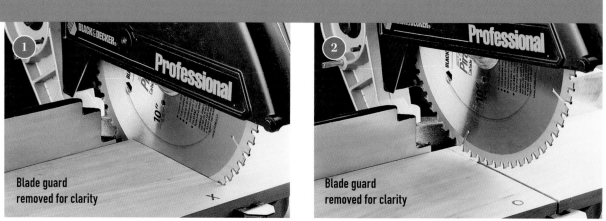

Blade guard removed for clarity

Blade guard removed for clarity

1   Make a full downward cut. Release the trigger and let the blade come to a full stop, then raise the saw arm.

2   Turn the workpiece over and carefully align the first cut with the saw blade. Make a second downward cut to finish the job.

USING A SLIDING MITER SAW

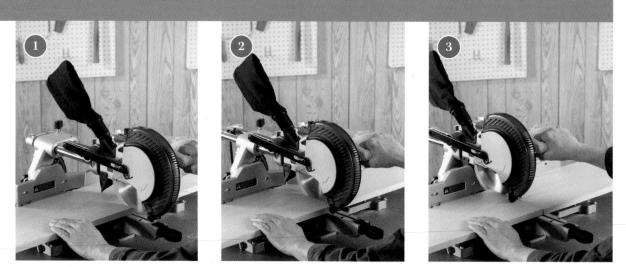

1   Sliding miter saws will cut with a plunge stroke, like a conventional miter saw. For wide workpieces, however, the saw's sliding arm allows it to also cut on a push stroke. First pull the saw toward yourself and align the blade with the cutting line. Start the saw to begin the cut, pivoting the blade down into the workpiece.

2   Push the blade carriage forward slowly until the workpiece has been cut through. Do not force the cut or the saw may kick back.

3   Once the piece is cut in two, stop the saw and wait until the blade stops before lifting it out of the workpiece.

MITER-CUTTING CASE MOLDINGS

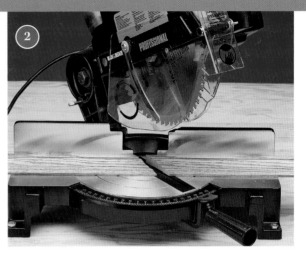

1   Mark cutting lines on each piece of molding or other material you plan to cut. On window and door casings, mark a line across the front face of the piece as a reference for the cutting direction. Remember: Only the beginning of the cutting line should actually be used to line up the saw blade. The freehand line across the face of the molding is a directional reference only.

2   Lay door and window casing stock flat on the saw bed and set the blade to match the cutting line. If you have a compound saw, set the bevel adjustment to 0°. Hold the casing with your hand at a safe distance from the blade, leaving the waste piece unsecured.

CUTTING BASEBOARDS

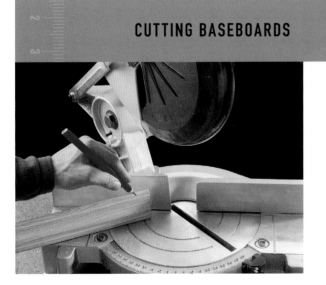

Mark a cutting line along the top edge of baseboards to indicate the starting point and direction for each cut. Baseboards and moldings that run the length of a wall are cut by standing the stock on-edge against the saw fence.

Join molding pieces for longer spans by mitering the ends at 45° angles. The mitered joint (scarf) cannot open up and show a crack if the wood shrinks.

1   On a non-compound miter saw, cove moldings must be positioned at an angle for cutting. Position the molding upside-down so the flats on the back of the molding are flush with the saw bed and fence.

2   Set the blade at 45° and cut the molding. To cut the molding for an adjoining wall, swivel the miter saw to the opposite 45° setting, and make a cut on the second piece that will fit with the first piece to form a corner.

Option

To miter cove molding on a compound miter saw, lay the molding flat on the saw bed and set the miter and bevel angles. For cove moldings, the standard settings are 33° (miter) and 31.62° (bevel). On many saws, these settings are highlighted for easy identification. If the walls are not perpendicular, you will need to experiment to find the correct settings.

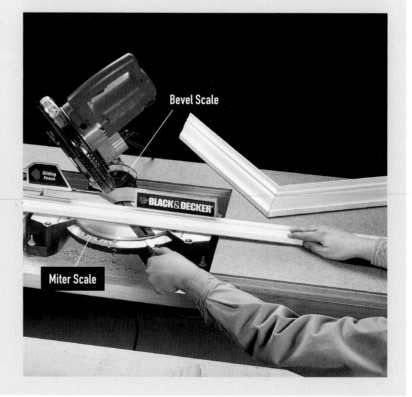

TABLE SAWS

For any serious do-it-yourself carpenter, a table saw is one of the most useful of all tools. Table saws make miter, rip, cross, and bevel cuts. They can also produce dadoes, dovetails, rabbets, and tenon joints for countless carpentry projects.

Several handmade accessories can improve your results and minimize the risk of injury when using a table saw. Pushsticks (page 49) make it easier to push stock through the blade's path while keeping your hands at a safe distance. Featherboards help keep your stock flat against the rip fence and table during cutting.

If you want to add a table saw to your workshop but don't have the money or enough space for a full-sized model, consider buying a portable table saw. Although they are smaller, these saws have most of the capabilities of a full-sized table saw.

For general carpentry work, use a combination blade. If you plan to do a lot of ripping or crosscutting and want the most accurate cuts possible, switch to a blade that's designed exclusively for that purpose.

The table saw is a versatile, highly accurate cutting tool. With virtually unlimited jigs and accessories available, such as this taper-cutting jig, there are very few cuts a table saw cannot make.

Safety Tip
Using a table saw requires extra caution because of the exposed position of the blade. Remember that your hands and fingers are vulnerable, even with a safety guard in place. Read the owner's manual for specific instructions on how to operate your saw. In the following photos, the blade guard and splitter have been removed for clarity.

USING A TABLE SAW

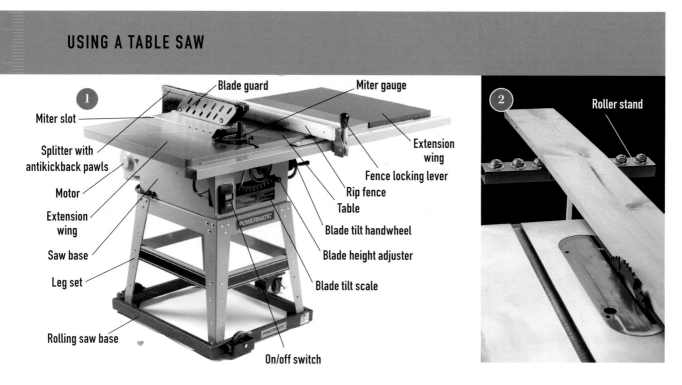

1   Learn what the parts and accessories of a table saw do before operating one. This contractor table saw includes: blade guard; rip fence, for aligning the cutting line on the workpiece with the blade; blade height adjuster and bevel angle scale; on/off switch; bevel tilt adjuster; and miter gauge, for setting miter angles.

2   Use a roller stand to hold long pieces of stock at the proper height when cutting them on a table saw. A roller stand allows you to slide the material across the table without letting the workpiece fall to the floor.

SETTING UP A TABLE SAW

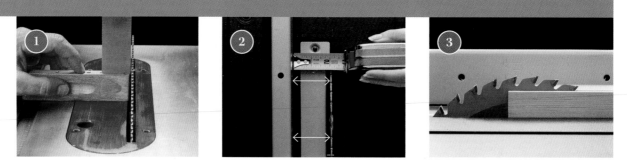

1   Check the vertical alignment of a table saw blade by adjusting the bevel to 0° and holding a try square against it. The blade and square must be flush. If not, adjust the blade according to the instructions in the owner's manual.

2   Check the horizontal blade alignment by measuring the distance between the blade and the rip fence at both ends of the blade. If the blade is not parallel to the fence, it may cause binding or kickback. Adjust the saw according to the owner's manual.

3   Set the blade so it extends no more than ½" above the surface of the workpiece. This minimizes strain on the motor and produces better cutting results.

CHANGING A TABLE SAW BLADE

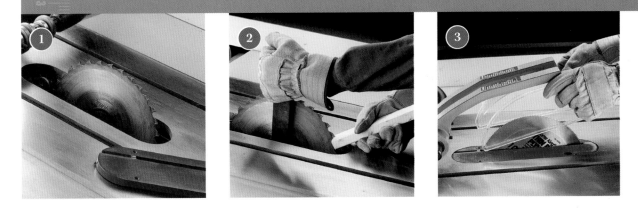

1   Unplug the table saw. Remove the blade guard and the table insert, then turn the blade height adjustment knob clockwise to raise the blade to its maximum height

2   Wearing gloves, hold the blade stationary with a piece of scrap wood. Loosen and remove the arbor nut. (An arbor wrench is supplied with most saws).

3   Carefully remove the old blade, and install the new blade so the teeth curve toward the front of the saw. Don't overtighten the arbor nut. Replace the table insert and the blade guard.

USING PUSHSTICKS & FEATHERBOARDS

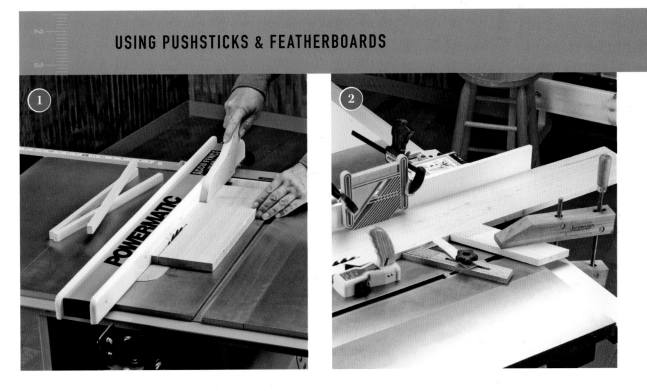

1   Pushsticks are essential safety items during rip cuts. They keep your hands clear of the blade.

2   Featherboards in various styles hold workpieces against the saw table or rip fence. They're especially useful for ripping long stock, where control can be difficult. Never use them on the outfeed side of the blade.

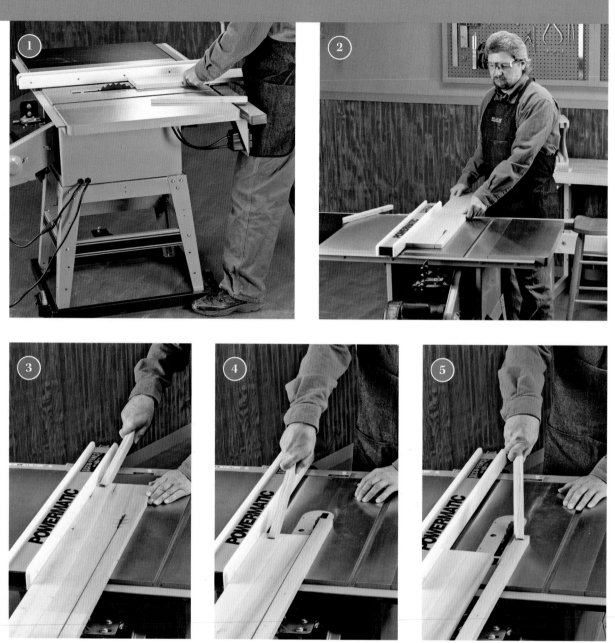

1   Start a rip cut by standing to the left of the workpiece, placing your left leg against the corner of the saw with your hip touching the front fence rail.

2   Feed the workpiece into the blade with your right hand while pressing the board against the fence with your left hand.

3   As you near the end of the cut, use a pushstick to feed the board past the blade.

4   When the board is cut in two, a waste piece will be left next to the blade. Don't reach for it by hand. Turn the saw off.

5   With the workpiece clear of the blade, use the pushstick to slide the waste piece away from the blade.

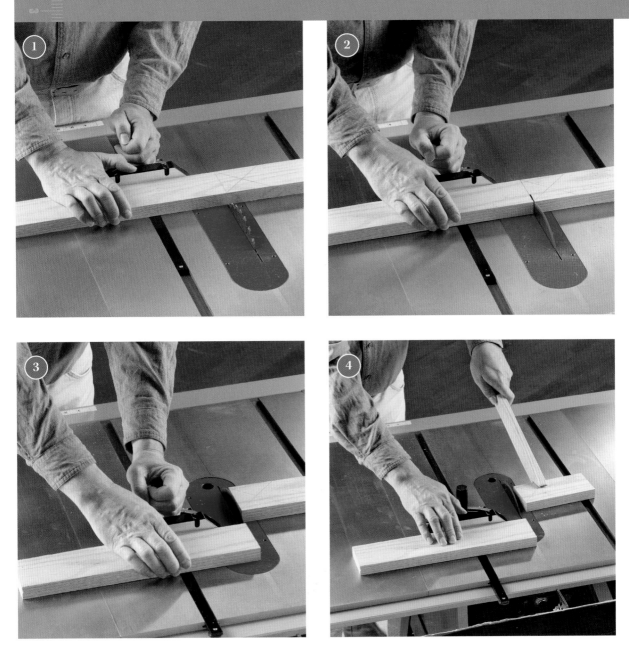

1   Align the blade carefully with the layout line before starting the saw and making the cut.

2   With the workpiece held firmly against the miter gauge, slide both past the blade to make the cut. Stand behind the miter gauge so your body is clear of the waste piece.

3   Push the miter gauge past the blade until the workpiece is cut in two and the workpiece is clear.

4   Slide the waste piece away from the blade with a pushstick. If it is too small to reach easily, turn off the saw first. Do not remove short waste pieces by hand with the saw running.

Using a Table Saw to Rip Sheet Goods

A table saw is a good choice for making clean, accurate cuts in plywood. Generally, it will produce better results than a circular saw. However, full-sized sheets of plywood can be unwieldly to handle and hard to lift up onto the saw table. The safest approach for cutting up large sheets is to cut them into smaller pieces first with a circular saw. Smaller sections will be much easier and safer to maneuver over the saw. Use extreme caution if a table saw is your only option for cutting up a full-sized sheet. To set up the cut, position a sturdy roller stand or shop table behind the saw to catch the plywood as it exits the blade. Make sure the outfeed support is slightly shorter than the saw table height to keep it from catching on workpieces during cutting. Install a general-purpose or fine-cutting blade. Set the blade height about ¼" higher than the plywood's thickness, and lock down the rip fence clamp.

Start the saw and tip the sheet up onto the saw table, making sure a long edge is flush against the rip fence. Stand along the opposite edge of the sheet near the back corner and push it into the blade. When the cut is underway, walk the sheet slowly into the blade and move around behind it to support the rear edge. Keep your hands clear as you complete the cut, pushing the section against the rip fence all the way past and clear of the blade. Turn off the saw and wait for the blade to stop before removing the workpieces.

RIPPING SHEET GOODS ON A TABLE SAW

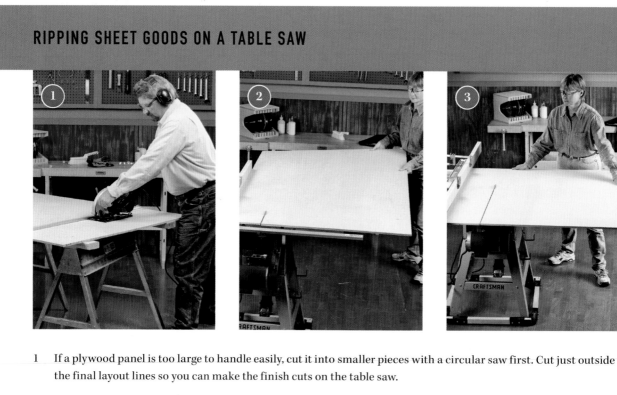

1   If a plywood panel is too large to handle easily, cut it into smaller pieces with a circular saw first. Cut just outside the final layout lines so you can make the finish cuts on the table saw.

2   Start the cut by standing behind the rear corner of the sheet and pushing with your right hand. Keep the material pressed firmly against the rip fence with your left hand. Slowly walk the sheet into the blade.

3   As the cut progresses, move your body behind the sheet to support the rear edge. Eventually, your right hand should push the material between the fence and blade all the way through the cut.

DRILLS & BITS

The power drill is one of the most popular and versatile power tools. Thanks to a host of improvements in its design, today's drills have many more functions than just drilling holes. Most have variable speed and reverse, making them convenient for driving and removing screws, nuts, and bolts, as well as for drilling, sanding, and stirring paint. A keyless chuck makes it easy to swap bits or quickly convert a drill into a grinder, sander, or paint mixer. Newer models allow you to adjust the drill's clutch for drilling or for driving into various materials, so the clutch will automatically disengage before screw heads strip or sink too far into the material.

Drills are commonly available in ¼-inch, ⅜-inch, and ½-inch sizes. The size refers to the maximum diameter of the bits and other accessories that the drill will accept. A ⅜-inch drill is standard for carpentry projects because it accepts a wide variety of bits and accessories and runs at a higher speed than ½-inch models.

Cordless technology has made drills more portable than ever. But it's important to understand the strengths of corded and cordless designs before deciding which one you should own. Most cordless drills operate at slower speeds and with less torque than corded models. Yet, cordless models are convenient because they allow up to several hours of operation between charges and eliminate the need for extension cords. Top-of-the-line cordless drills generate about 1,200 rpm. Corded drills weigh significantly less because they don't require battery packs, and some operate at more than 2,000 rpm. For most jobs, a cordless drill's slower speed is not a problem, but as the battery wears down, drilling becomes difficult and more of a strain on the motor. Spare battery packs can offset this problem. If you own both types of drills, keep your corded model on hand as a backup.

Shopping for Drills

When shopping for a drill, remember that the most powerful tool is not necessarily the best one for the job. This is especially true of cordless drills, because

Drills include: (A) Clutch adjustment dial, (B) Variable speed switch, (C) Screw bit holder, (D) Keyless chuck, (E) Trigger lock and reversing switch, (F) Voltage rating, (G) Battery pack.

higher voltage ratings usually require heavier batteries. A more powerful cordless model is useful for heavy-duty drilling, when extra power will allow you to drill holes in thick timbers or masonry more quickly and easily. For driving screws and for light-duty drilling, a medium-voltage cordless model or a corded drill is a better choice. A drill in the 12- to 14.4-volt range is usually sufficient for most tasks. Try out several drills so you can compare the feel of the tools under load.

You'll also appreciate having two battery packs to minimize waiting for recharging. Most good-quality cordless drills come with one-hour chargers.

Skillbuilder

Using a cordless drill with an adjustable clutch, drive a series of drywall or deck screws fully into scrap lumber. Drive the first screw with the clutch set at the lowest setting. Increase the clutch setting with each screw until you reach the highest. Drive a screw with the clutch set on drill. If you have a corded variable speed drill, repeat the same exercise with the corded drill. Notice how the lack of a clutch leads to stripping out more screwheads.

Corded drills are still widely available because they can generate lots of torque and operate at speeds of 2,000 rpm or more. If you want a fast, powerful, lightweight drill, a corded drill may be the right tool for you.

A hammer drill combines the rotary motion of a conventional drill with the impact action of a hammer. It can drill holes in masonry much faster than a regular drill. Hammer drills can also be set for rotary motion only, making them useful for general drilling applications.

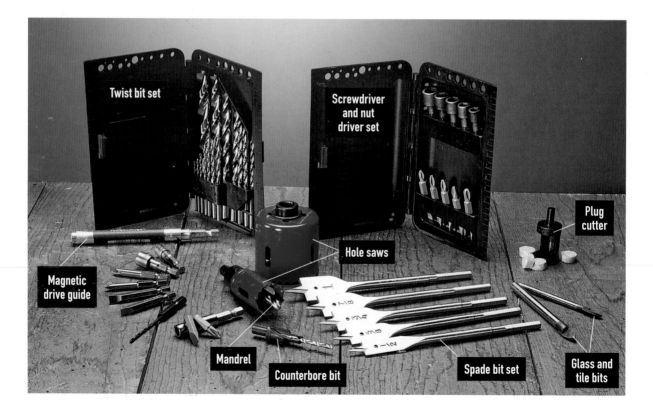

Drill bits include: a magnetic drive guide, twist bit set, screwdriver and nut driver set, plug cutter, glass and tile bits, spade bit set, hole saw bits, and adjustable counterbore bit. These accessories are often sold with a drill or are available separately.

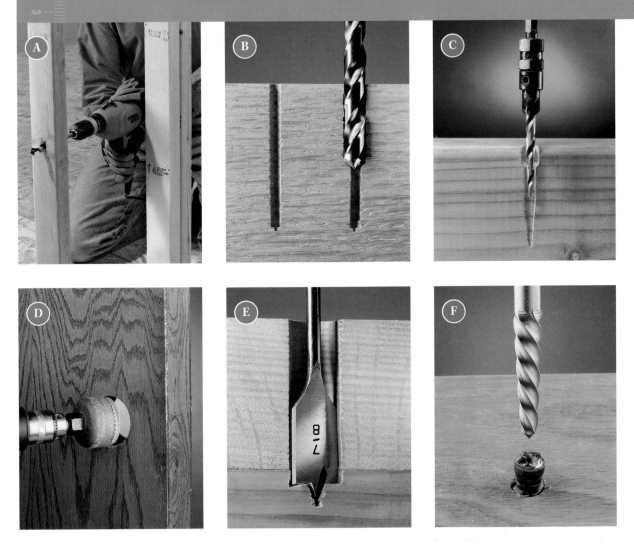

A   An auger bit is designed with a screw-like tip and deep threads. It bores raceway holes for wiring quickly and easily by self-feeding through the wood.

B   Twist bits are used for general hole boring. In hardwood, drill a pilot hole first. The extra step will prevent binding and splintering as the larger bit cuts through the wood.

C   Use an adjustable counterbore bit to drill pilot, countersink, and counterbore holes with one action. Loosen the setscrew to match the bit to the size and shape of the screw.

D   Drill holes for door knobs and cylinders with a hole saw. To prevent the door from splintering, drill until the hole saw pilot (mandrel) just comes through the other side of the door. Complete the hole from the opposite side.

E   A spade bit is used for larger diameter holes in wood. Use a backerboard when drilling holes in hardwood and finish plywood or any time you want to prevent blemishes. A backerboard placed on the bottom of the workpiece prevents splintering as the bit breaks through.

F   Remove a broken screw by drilling a pilot hole in the top of the screw and removing it with a properly sized, reverse-thread extracting bit.

SANDERS

Power sanding tools shape and smooth wood and other building materials in preparation for painting and finishing. Carpenters also use them for removing small amounts of material. Finish sanders (opposite page, top) are best for light to medium sanding and for achieving very smooth surfaces. Belt sanders (opposite page, bottom left) are suitable for most work involving rough, fast removal of material. For very small, intricate, or contoured areas, sand by hand with folded sandpaper or a sanding block, or use drill-mounted sanding accessories (opposite page, bottom right).

When sanding a rough workpiece that requires a fine finish, begin sanding with a lower-grit sandpaper. Slowly move up to a higher grit to achieve the finish you want. Medium sanding jobs normally consist of three sanding steps: coarse, medium, and fine.

Sanding is painstaking work. Take your time and do it right the first time. If you attempt to cut corners when sanding a project, you will see it in the end result.

Tip
Sanders create airborne particles of material. Consider buying a sander that has a dust collection bag, and always wear a dust mask and eye protection.

Use a power sander to remove unwanted material and create a smooth finish. This random-orbit sander is used in general applications that require medium to heavy sanding. The orbital motion combines a circular pattern with side-to-side motion. Unlike disc sanders, random orbit sanders leave no circular markings, and there's no need to follow the grain of the wood. Sanding discs are available with hook-and-loop fasteners or pressure-sensitive adhesive. Sponge applicators and accessories are also available for buffing.

Finish sanders are designed for jobs that require medium- to light-duty sanding to achieve a fine finish. Types of finish sanders include: (A) 3-in-1 sander for finish sanding, medium material removal, and detail work; (B) traditional finish sander for finishing larger areas; (C) palm sander for detail work; and (D) detail sander for smaller-scale finish work and easy corner access. The palm sander is also ideal for polishing and scrubbing jobs when fitted with the appropriate accessories.

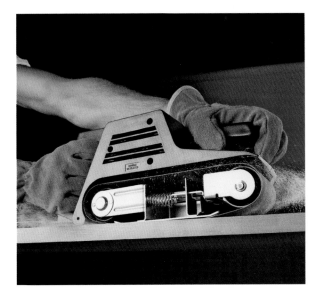

Remove material from large areas quickly with a belt sander. Disposable belts are available ranging from 36 (extra-coarse) to 100 (fine) grit. Most belt sanding is done with the grain. However, sanding across the grain is an effective way to remove material from rough-hewn lumber.

Sanding accessories for power drills include (clockwise from top right): disc sander for fast sanding, sanding drums, and flap sanders to smooth contoured surfaces.

A Sanding station. A disk sander's flat table and miter gauge make it helpful for sanding edges flat and square. Tip the miter gauge to refine angled workpieces, such as mitered trim. For best accuracy, sand up to a marked layout line.

B Drum sander. It's possible to sand broad curves using a belt or random-orbital sander, but use a drum sander mounted in a drill press or power drill for sanding tight curves.

C Clean sandpaper with a stiff-bristle brush to remove sawdust and grit that can clog the sandpaper and reduce its effectiveness.

D It's often faster to start heavy stock removal with a coarse rasp, then switch to a sander when most of the stock is filed away. A rasp will not create airborne sawdust, so it is also a cleaner tool to use. Wear gloves if you need to hold the rasp by the blade. Notice that a rasp cuts on the push stroke only.

E A sanding block is helpful for smoothing flat surfaces. For curved areas, wrap sandpaper around a folded piece of scrap carpeting or 2 × 4.

F When sanding the edge of a board with a belt sander, clamp it between two pieces of scrap lumber to prevent the belt sander from wobbling and rounding off the edges.

A   Use 60-grit coarse sandpaper on hardwood flooring and to grind down badly scratched surfaces.

B   Use 100-grit sandpaper for initial smoothing of wood. Move the sander in the direction of the wood grain to achieve the smoothest surface.

C   Use 150-, then 180-grit fine sandpaper to put a smooth finish on wood surfaces. Fine sandpaper will prepare wood surfaces for staining or smooth drywall joints.

D   Use 220-grit extra-fine sandpaper to smooth stained wood before staining. Use 400-grit and higher sandpaper between coats of varnish.

PNEUMATIC NAILERS

Nail guns use compressed air, other gas, or a battery to drive nails into wood. The air-powered—or pneumatic—nail guns offer many advantages over hand-nailing, for both novices and professional carpenters alike. For one, the guns are simple and efficient to use. Rather than swinging a hammer several times to drive and set a nail, a nail gun completes the whole task in one trigger squeeze. Position the gun's tip where you want the nail to be, press down the safety on the nailing tip, and squeeze the trigger to fire the nail. The process is the same, whether you're driving a tiny brad or a 3-inch framing nail. Most professional carpenters use nail guns because large framing or trim carpentry jobs can be completed in much less time than hand-nailing.

Nail guns will help improve your nailing accuracy. You'll never need to worry about a glanced hammer blow denting the wood or bending a nail. Air nailers never miss the nail head. As long as you choose the correct nails for the application and set the air compressor pressure properly, a pneumatic nailer will drive and set nails reliably, time after time.

Nail guns are made in various sizes to suit different carpentry applications. Framing nailers are designed to drive large-shank nails through framing lumber. Brad nailers drive smaller, casing-sized nails for installing trim moldings. Roofing nailers tack shingles in place using long coils of collated nails, sometimes with washers on the shanks. There are even nail guns made for attaching metal joist hanger hardware and strapping. Most styles are available for rent if you only need a nail gun for occasional projects.

When using a nail gun, you'll usually need a tank-style air compressor to supply the air. Set the air pressure correctly for the gun you're using. Most nailers require around 60 to 100 psi of continuous pressure to operate. Use the correct style and sizes of nails for the gun—some nail styles are not interchangeable from one nailer to the next. Also, add a few drops of nail gun oil into the air nozzle to lubricate the internal drive mechanism if your gun requires it. Always wear ear and eye protection when operating a nail gun.

Unlike some other pneumatic tools, nail guns don't require a large air compressor or high volume of air to operate properly. A 4-gallon compressor is generally adequate. Compressors are made in several styles, including single tank, twin-tank, and pancake varieties. Some are equipped to power more than one nailer at a time.

Framing nailers are ideal for assembling wall, floor, and roof framework. They're the largest nail guns for home carpentry, capable of driving 2 to 4" framing nails.

Brad nailers are designed for attaching baseboard, wall moldings, and window and door casings. Some styles have angled magazines that make it easier to work in tight spaces and corners.

Coil roofing nailers install shingles or wall sheathing quickly and easily. The round magazine stores longer clips of nails than a straight magazine for improved efficiency. These guns can be fired repeatedly by holding the trigger and tapping the gun along the work surface.

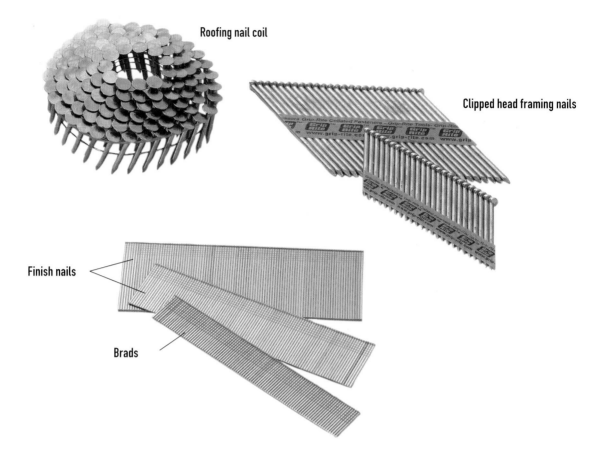

Roofing nail coil

Clipped head framing nails

Finish nails

Brads

Pneumatic nails are made in a variety of styles, sizes, and compositions to suit specific tasks. Clips are either straight or angled, and framing nail heads can be round or clipped. You can buy uncoated or galvanized nails as well as nails designed for use with treated lumber or marine applications.

To prepare a nail gun for use, slide a clip of nails down into the slot in the magazine and close the cover. Add a few drops of oil into the air hose nozzle, if necessary, before each use.

Drive a nail by positioning the gun's nailing tip where you want the nail to be and pushing the safety tip against the workpiece. Hold the gun firmly and squeeze the trigger. Lift the gun off to re-engage the safety.

Adjust the air compressor's regulator to achieve the recommended air pressure for the gun you're using. Incorrect air pressure will cause the nailer to either overdrive the nails or stop them short of setting properly.

POWDER-ACTUATED TOOLS

Occasionally, your carpentry projects may involve fastening wood to metal or concrete, such as attaching wall sole plates to concrete floors. You may even need to fasten metal plumbing straps or conduit clips to steel I-beams. In these situations, you could use hardened screws for fastening, but that involves lots of tedious drilling and usually a few broken or stripped screw heads. An easier alternative is to use small charges of gunpowder to drive hardened nails into metal or concrete with a powder-actuated nail gun.

Powder-actuated nailers look and work a bit like a pile driver or handgun. A steel barrel holds specially designed, hardened nails called drive pins. The nails are equipped with a plastic sleeve to keep them centered in the barrel. Driving force is delivered by a small gunpowder charge, called a power load, which looks like a rifle shell with a crimped tip. The power loads fit into a magazine behind the barrel on the tool. Squeezing the tool's trigger, or hitting the end with a hammer (depending on the tool style), activates a firing pin that ignites the gunpowder. The expanding gasses drive a piston against the nail at great force. Powder-actuated nailers can drive only one fastener at a time, but some styles will hold a clip of multiple power loads for faster operation.

Power loads are made in a range of color-coded calibers to suit different nailing applications and drive pin sizes. Follow the manufacturer's recommendations carefully to choose the correct load and fastener for your task. Generally, the safest method is to start with the lowest energy load that will work for your nailing situation and see if it's sufficient to fully drive the nail. Use the next stronger load, if necessary.

Powder-actuated nailers are easy to use for do-it-yourselfers and safe for indoor projects, provided you wear hearing and eye protection and follow all manufacturer's instructions. Most home centers sell the nail guns and supplies, or you can rent these tools.

Powder-actuated nailers offer the quickest and easiest method for fastening framing to block and concrete.

Powder-actuated nail guns (PATs) are designed in two styles. Plunger types are activated by hitting the end of the shaft with a hammer, while trigger styles function like a handgun. With either type, the barrel must be depressed against the work surface to release a safety before a drive pin can be fired.

Powder loads contain various amounts of gunpowder inside a crimped shell. Color coding ensures that you're using the right amount of charge for your drive pin size and the materials you're fastening together. Follow the color charts carefully, starting with a low-powder charge.

PATs use hardened nails, called drive pins, in a range of sizes. A plastic finned sleeve centers the drive pin in the tool barrel.

USING A POWDER-ACTUATED TOOL

1 To prepare a PAT for use, slide a drive pin into the barrel first. Push it in until the nail tip is flush with the end of the barrel. Be sure there's no powder load in the magazine.

2 Slide the magazine open and insert a powder load into the barrel. A rim on the load shell ensures that it can only be loaded one way. Close the magazine.

3 Press the end of the barrel firmly against the work surface to release the safety. Squeeze the trigger or strike the end of the tool sharply with a hammer to fire the drive pin. Once the pin is fired, slide open the magazine to eject the spent load shell.

Tip
Occasionally, your first powder load selection won't completely set the nail. In these situations, use a hand maul to drive it in the rest of the way. Choose a stronger powder load for driving subsequent fasteners.

ROUTERS

Among workshop tools, the router is the undisputed king of versatility. With a router, you can cut, shape edges, build joints, create decorative inlays, and even drill holes. More research and development goes into router innovations each year than virtually any other woodworking tool. And for all these various capabilities, routers don't cost a fortune. A good-quality router is worth every cent you pay.

The two main types of routers for general workshop use are fixed-base and plunge. A third type, called a trim router, is a much smaller tool primarily used to trim plastic laminate.

Fixed-base routers are the standard-issue tools of the router family. They have a motor that's adjusted up or down on its base and is fixed in place for the routing operation. Standard fixed-base models range in power from 1½ to 2¼ horsepower and are suitable for most handheld and table routing jobs. Large fixed-base tools, with 3 horsepower or more, are called heavy-duty, or production, routers and are used for heavy work with large bits. They also make excellent table routers.

Plunge routers have a special base that allows the motor to travel up and down while under power. This feature lets you plunge the spinning router bit down into the workpiece, move the tool sideways for a horizontal cut, then retract the bit from the wood at the end of the cut. Plunge routers can do everything standard fixed-base routers can do but are especially useful for inside cuts, such as mortises.

The plunge router (left) and fixed base router (right) are the two main types of routers for general workshop use. A trim router (center) is smaller and used primarily for trimming plastic laminate.

Router Kits. Many manufacturers now make router kits that consist of a motor and both plunge (left) and fixed (right) bases.

Plunge Routers. For some router operations, like cutting hinge mortises or template routing, a plunge router offers more convenience than a fixed-base router.

A flush-trimming bit with a bottom bearing rides along a template placed below the workpiece.

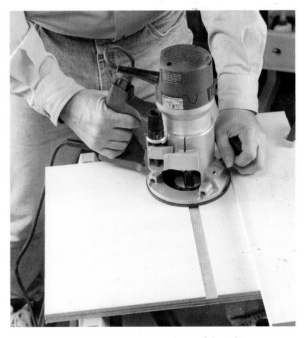

To cut a dado with a router, use a straight bit the same diameter as the dado width. Clamp a guide block to the work piece and make the cut in several passes of increasing depth.

BASIC CARPENTRY

OBVIOUSLY, ADDING A SECOND floor to your home is an advanced project that most homeowners are not going to attempt. However, finishing a basement is a fairly common do-it-yourself project. To do so you'll need to know how to build a partition wall, frame a door, and perhaps trim a window. All it takes is a set of clear instructions, a little patience, and practice.

The medium of carpentry is lumber, so it is good to know what is available and how to use it. Dimensional lumber, sheet goods, and trim are all covered in the following chapter. In addition, the fasteners and adhesives needed to put it all together are shown.

Contact your local building inspector to see if your project requires a permit.

LUMBER

Lumber for structural applications such as walls, floors, and ceilings is usually milled from strong softwoods and is categorized by grade, moisture content, and dimension.

Grade: Characteristics such as knots, splits, and grain slope affect the strength of the lumber and determine the grade (chart, opposite page).

Moisture content: Lumber is also categorized by moisture content. S-DRY (surfaced dry) is the designation for lumber with a moisture content of 19 percent or less. S-DRY lumber is the least likely to warp or shrink and is a good choice for framing walls. S-GRN (surfaced green) means the lumber contains a moisture content of 19 percent or more.

Exterior lumber: Lumber milled from redwood or cedar is naturally resistant to decay and insect infestation and is a good choice for exterior applications. The most durable part of a tree is the heartwood, so specify heartwood for pieces that will be in contact with the ground.

Treated lumber: Lumber injected with chemicals under pressure is resistant to decay and is generally less expensive than decay-resistant heartwoods such as redwood and cedar. For outdoor structures like decks, use treated lumber for posts and joists and more attractive redwood or cedar for decks and railings.

Dimension lumber: Lumber is sold according to its nominal size, such as 2 × 4. Its actual size (chart, page 73) is smaller. Always use actual sizes for measuring and estimating.

Check lumber visually before buying it. Take the time to choose the boards with the fewest defects, even if they will be hidden behind wall surfaces.

The Steel-Framing Alternative

Lumber is not the only material available for framing walls. Metal studs and tracks offer an attractive—if less common—choice for new construction. Steel-framed walls can be installed faster than wood stud walls—the parts are attached by crimping and screwing the flanges—and the channels are precut to accommodate electrical and plumbing lines. Steel framing is also lighter in weight, easy to recycle, fireproof, and comparable in price to lumber. If you are interested in using steel framing for a new wall in a wood-framed home, consult a professional for information about electrical, plumbing, and load-bearing safety precautions. Steel framing is available at most home centers.

Much of today's lumber is still fairly wet when it is sold, so it's hard to predict how it will behave as it dries. But a quick inspection of each board at the lumberyard or home center will help you disqualify flawed boards. Lumber that is cupped, twisted, or crooked should not be used at full length. However, you may be able to cut out good sections for use as blocking or other short framing pieces. If a board is slightly bowed, you can probably flatten it out as you nail it. Checks, wanes, and knots are cosmetic flaws that seldom affect the strength of the board. The exception is a knot that is loose or missing. In this case, cut off the damaged area. Sections with splits should also be cut off. Splits are likely to spread as the wood dries.

Grade	Description, uses
Clear	Free of knots and defects
SEL STR or Select Structural	Good appearance, strength, and stiffness
1, 2, 3	1, 2, 3 grades indicate knot size
CONST or Construction	Both grades used for general framing
STAND or Standard	Good strength and serviceability
STUD or Stud	Special designation used in any stud application, including load-bearing walls
UTIL or Utility	Economical choice for blocking and bracing

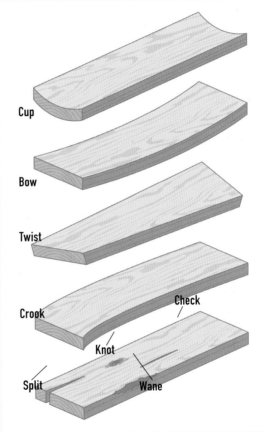

Cup

Bow

Twist

Crook

Check

Knot

Split

Wane

Grade stamps provide valuable information about a piece of lumber. The lumber's grade is usually indicated by the largest number stamped on the wood. Also stamped on each piece of lumber are its moisture content, species, and lumber mill of origin.

Picking the right wood for a project is a decision that will affect the durability and attractiveness of the final product. Some woods are more prone to warping than others, some are more resistant to decay, and some are superior when it comes to accepting a coat of paint. Matching styles and wood varieties will help to create a common theme throughout your home.

Lumber sizes such as 2 × 4 are nominal dimensions, not actual dimensions. The actual size of lumber is slightly smaller than the nominal size. When it is originally milled, lumber is cut at the nominal size; however, the boards are then planed down for a smoother finish, producing the actual dimensions you buy in the store. See the chart on the opposite page for nominal and actual dimensions.

Softwood	Description	Uses
Cedar	Easy to cut, holds paint well. Heartwood resists decay.	Decks, shakes, shingles, posts, and other decay-prone surfaces.
Fir, larch	Stiff, hard wood. Holds nails well. Some varieties are hard to cut.	Framing materials, flooring, and subflooring.
Pine	Lightweight, soft wood with a tendency to shrink. Holds nails well. Some varieties resist decay.	Paneling, trim, siding, and decks.
Redwood	Lightweight, soft wood that holds paint well. Easy to cut. Heartwood resists decay and insect damage.	Outdoor applications, such as decks, posts, and fences.
Treated lumber	Chemically treated to resist decay. Use corrosion-resistant fasteners only. Wear protective eye wear and clothing to avoid skin, lung, and eye irritation.	Ground-contact and other outdoor applications where resistance to decay is important.

Hardwood	Description	Uses
Birch	Hard, strong wood that is easy to cut and holds paint well.	Painted cabinets, trim, and plywood.
Maple	Heavy, hard, strong wood that is difficult to cut with hand tools.	Flooring, furniture, and countertops.
Poplar	Soft, light wood that is easy to cut with hand or power tools.	Painted cabinets, trim, tongue-and-groove paneling, and plywood cores.
Oak	Heavy, hard, strong wood that is difficult to cut with hand tools.	Furniture, flooring, doors, and trim.
Walnut	Heavy, hard, strong wood that is easy to cut.	Fine woodwork, paneling, and mantelpieces.

Type	Description	Common Nominal Sizes	Actual Sizes
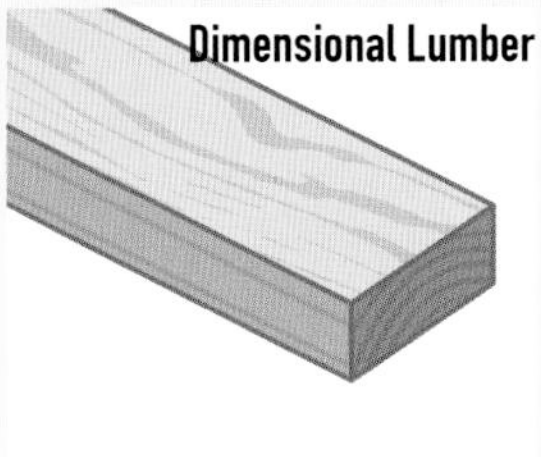 **Dimensional Lumber**	Used in framing of walls, ceilings, floors, rafters, structural finishing, exterior decking, fencing, and stairs.	1×4 1×6 1×8 2×2 2×4 2×6 2×8	¾" × 3½" ¾" × 5½" ¾" × 7¼" 1½" × 1½" 1½" × 3½" 1½" × 5½" 1½" × 7¼"
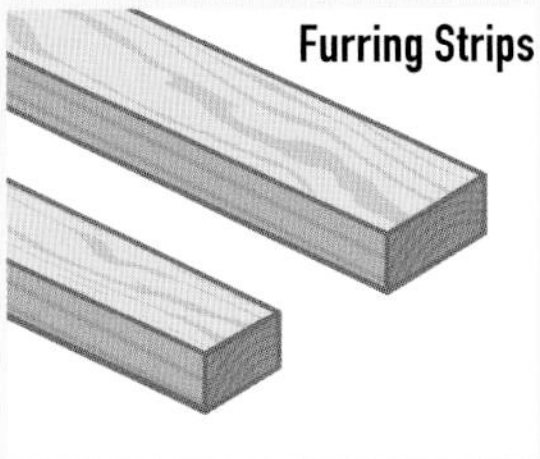 **Furring Strips**	Used in framing of walls, ceilings, floors, rafters, structural finishing, exterior decking, fencing, and stairs.	1×2 1×4	¾" × 1½" ¾" × 2½"
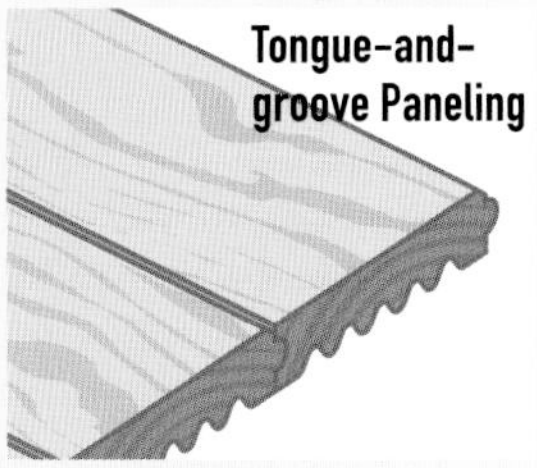 **Tongue-and-groove Paneling**	Used in wainscoting and full-length paneling of walls and ceilings.	$\frac{5}{16}$" × 4 1×4 1×6 1×8	Varies, depending on milling process and application.
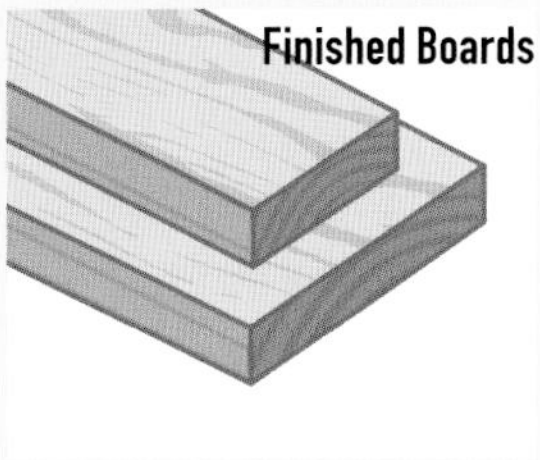 **Finished Boards**	Used in trim, shelving, cabinetry, and other applications where a fine finish is required.	1×4 1×6 1×8 1×10 1×12	¾" × 3½" ¾" × 5½" ¾" × 7½" ¾" × 9½" ¾" × 11½"
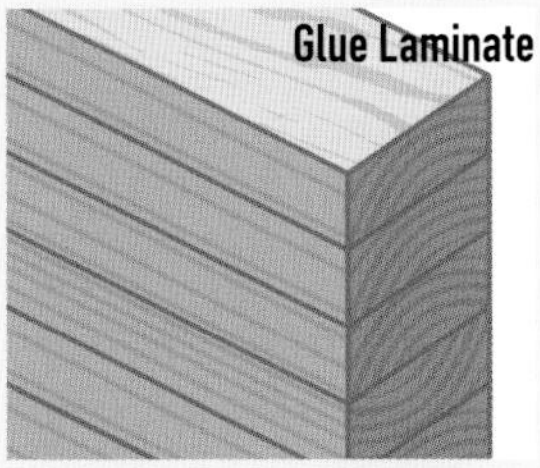 **Glue Laminate**	Composed of layers of lumber laminated to form a solid piece. Used for beams and joists.	4×10 4×12 6×10 6×12	3½" × 9 3½" × 12 3½" × 9 3½" × 12
Micro-lam	Composed of thin layers glued together for use in joists and beams.	4×12	3½" × 11⅜"

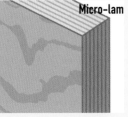

PLYWOOD & SHEET GOODS

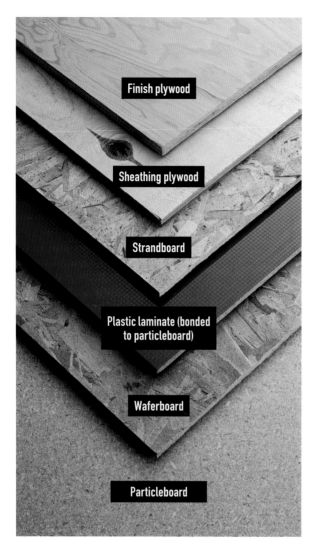

There are many different types of sheet goods, but plywood is the most widely used. Plywood is an extremely versatile sheet material that is made up of thinly sliced layers or plies of wood. Plywood is available in thicknesses ranging from ³⁄₁₆" to ¾" and is graded A through D, depending on the quality of the wood in its outer plies. It is also graded for interior or exterior usage. Classifications for plywood are based on the wood species used for the face and back veneers. Group 1 species are the strongest and stiffest, Group 2 is the next strongest.

Finish plywood is graded either A-C, meaning it has a finish-quality wood veneer on one side and a utility-grade ply on the other side, or A-A, indicating it has a finish veneer on both sides.

Sheathing plywood is graded C-D with two rough sides and features a bond between plies that is waterproof. Plywood rated EXPOSURE 1 is for use where some moisture is present, and plywood rated EXTERIOR is used in applications that are permanently exposed to weather. Sheathing plywood also carries a thickness rating and a roof and floor span index, which appear as two numbers separated by a diagonal slash. The first number, for roofing application, indicates the maximum spacing

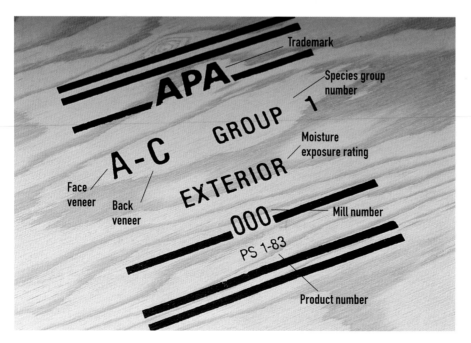

The finish plywood grading stamp shows the grade of face and back veneers, species group number, and a moisture exposure rating. Mill numbers and product numbers are for the manufacturer's use.

for rafters. The second number specifies the joist spacing when plywood is used for subflooring. Some plywood is stamped "sized for spacing." This means that the actual dimensions are slightly smaller than 4 × 8 feet to allow space for expansion between sheets after installation.

Plastic laminates make durable surfaces for countertops and furniture. Plastic laminates are sometimes bonded to particleboard for use in shelving, cabinets, and countertops.

Strand-, particle-, and waferboard are made from waste chips or inexpensive wood species and are used for shelving and floor underlayment.

Foam insulating board is lightweight and serves as insulation for basement walls.

Water-resistant drywall is used behind ceramic wall tiles and in other high-moisture areas.

Drywall, also known as wallboard, Sheetrock, and plasterboard, comes in panels 4-feet wide, 2-, 4-, 8-, 10-, or 12-feet long, and in ⅜-inch, ½-inch, and ⅝-inch thicknesses.

Pegboard and hardboard are made from wood fibers and resins bonded together under high pressure and are used for tool organization with a workbench and as shelf backing.

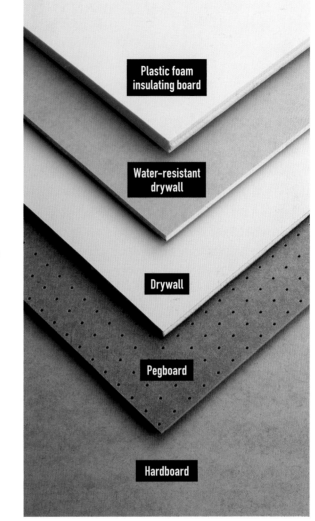

Plastic foam insulating board

Water-resistant drywall

Drywall

Pegboard

Hardboard

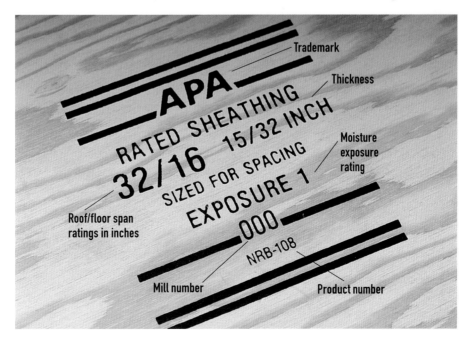

The sheathing plywood grading stamp shows thickness, roof or floor span index, and exposure rating, in addition to the manufacturer's information.

Trademark

Thickness

APA

RATED SHEATHING

32/16   15/32 INCH

SIZED FOR SPACING

EXPOSURE 1

000

NRB-108

Roof/floor span ratings in inches

Moisture exposure rating

Mill number

Product number

TRIM MOLDINGS

Trim moldings give character and definition to many carpentry projects. In addition, you can sometimes use them to cover up carpentry mistakes, such as hiding small gaps in wall corners when the drywall hasn't been cut perfectly.

It's important to measure and cut moldings precisely so that when installed, they fit together snugly without gaps. Predrilling moldings is recommended, especially when hardwoods such as oak are used. Predrilling makes hand nailing easier, reduces splitting during installation, and makes it easier to set nails cleanly. There's no need to predrill when using a pneumatic nail gun.

Most moldings should be painted or stained before installation. Cove moldings and wainscoting can be purchased with a factory coat of white paint. Pine and poplar are good choices if you plan to paint. For stained surfaces, use a hardwood with a pleasing grain, such as oak.

Tip
Use the same wood species whenever possible in selecting trim materials for walls, doors, and windows. Even when painted, oak shows a distinct grain pattern that painted poplar does not have.

Decorative moldings give a finished appearance to walls, doors, windows, and cabinets.

Trim moldings are both functional and decorative. They can be used to conceal gaps at the base and around the sides of a carpentry project, to hide the edges of plywood surfaces, or simply to add visual interest to the project. Moldings are available in dozens of styles, but the samples shown here are widely available at all home improvement centers.

Synthetic trim moldings, available in many styles, are less expensive than hardwood moldings. Synthetic moldings are made of wood composites (A) or rigid foam (B) covered with a layer of melamine.

Baseboard molding (C) is used to trim the bottom edge of a wall along the floor line. Choosing molding that matches the baseboard elsewhere in your home helps your project fit in with its surroundings.

Hardwood strips (D) are used to construct face frames for carpentry projects and to cover unfinished edges of plywood shelves. Maple, oak, and poplar strips are widely available in 1×2, 1×3, and 1×4 sizes.

Crown moldings (E, F) cover gaps between the top of a wall and the ceiling. They can also add a decorative accent to other projects.

Cove molding (G) is a simple, unobtrusive trim for covering gaps.

Ornamental moldings, including spindle and rail (H) and embossed moldings (I, J), give a distinctive look to many projects.

Door-edge molding (K), also called cap molding, is only available in specialty stores in some areas. It is used with finish-grade plywood to create panel-style doors and drawer faces.

Shelf-edge molding (L), also called base cap molding, provides a decorative edge to plywood shelves or can be used to create a wider baseboard molding.

Base-shoe molding (M) covers gaps around the top, bottom, and sides of a wall. Because it bends easily, base-shoe molding works well to cover irregular gaps caused by uneven walls and loose floors.

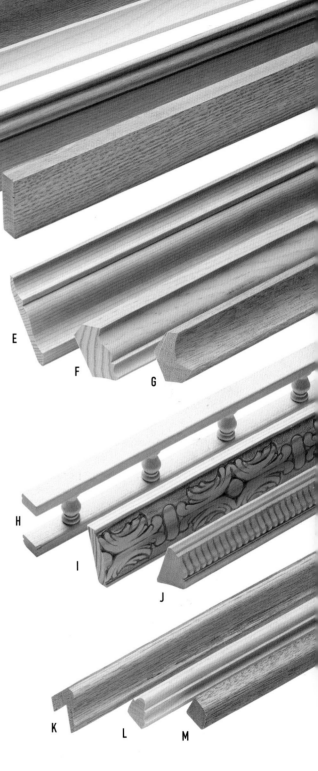

NAILS

The wide variety of nail styles and sizes makes it possible to choose exactly the right fastener for each job. Nails are identified by their typical purpose, such as casing, flooring, or roofing nails; or by a physical feature, such as galvanized, coated, or spiral. Some nails come in both a galvanized and non-galvanized version. Use galvanized nails for outdoor projects and non-galvanized indoors. Nail lengths may be specified in inches or by numbers from 4 to 60 followed by the letter "d," which stands for "penny" (see "Nail Sizes," opposite page).

Some of the most popular nails for carpentry projects include:

- Common and box nails for general framing work. Box nails are smaller in diameter, which makes them less likely to split wood. Box nails were designed for constructing boxes and crates, but they can be used in any application where thin, dry wood will be nailed close to the edge of the piece. Most common and box nails have a cement or vinyl coating that improves their holding power.
- Finish and casing nails, which have small heads and are driven just below the work surface with a nail set. Finish nails are used for attaching moldings and other trim to walls. Casing nails are used for nailing window and door casings. They have a slightly larger head than finish nails for better holding power.
- Brads, or small wire nails sometimes referred to as finish nails. They are used primarily in cabinetry, where very small nail holes are preferred.
- Flooring nails, which are often spiral-shanked for extra holding power to prevent floorboards from separating or squeaking. Spiral flooring nails are sometimes used in other applications, such as installing tongue-and-groove paneling on ceilings.
- Galvanized nails, which have a zinc coating that resists rusting. They are used for outdoor projects.
- Drywall nails, once the standard fastener for drywall, are less common today because of the development of Phillips-head drywall screws that drive quickly with a screw gun or drill and offer superior holding power (page 80).

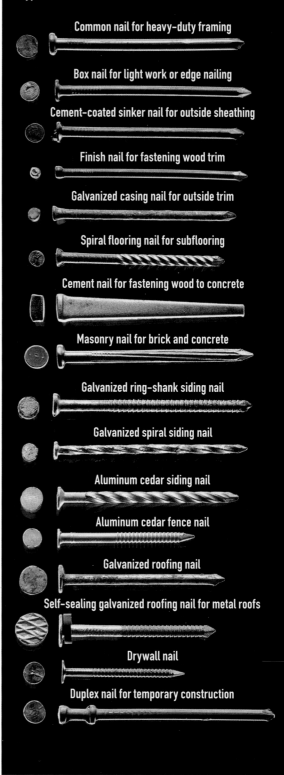

Types of Nails

Common nail for heavy-duty framing

Box nail for light work or edge nailing

Cement-coated sinker nail for outside sheathing

Finish nail for fastening wood trim

Galvanized casing nail for outside trim

Spiral flooring nail for subflooring

Cement nail for fastening wood to concrete

Masonry nail for brick and concrete

Galvanized ring-shank siding nail

Galvanized spiral siding nail

Aluminum cedar siding nail

Aluminum cedar fence nail

Galvanized roofing nail

Self-sealing galvanized roofing nail for metal roofs

Drywall nail

Duplex nail for temporary construction

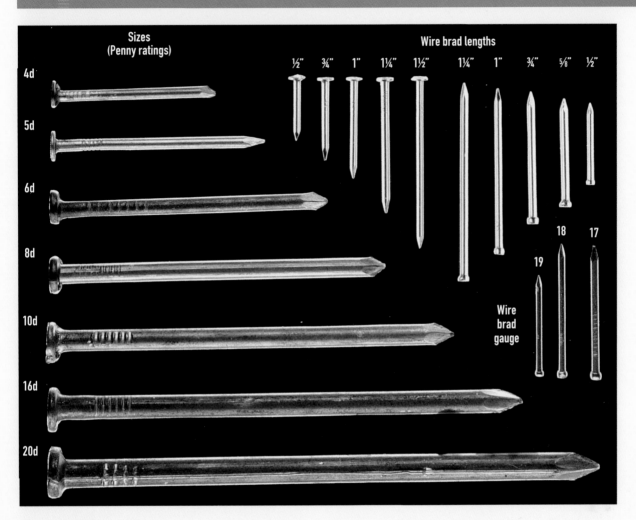

The pennyweight scale that manufacturers use to size nails was developed centuries ago as an approximation of the number of pennies it would take to buy 100 nails of that size. The range of nail types available today (and what they cost) is much wider, but the scale is still in use. Each pennyweight refers to a specific length (see chart, below), although you will find slight variations in length from one nail type to the next. For example, box nails of a given pennyweight are roughly ⅛" shorter than common nails of the same weight.

Estimating Nail Quantities

Estimate the number of nails you'll need for a project, then use the chart to determine approximately how many pounds of nails to purchase.

Note: Sizes and quantities not listed are less common, although they may be available through some manufacturers.

	Pennyweight	2d	3d	4d	5d	6d	7d	8d	10d	12d	16d	20d
	Length (in.)	1	1¼	1½	1⅝	2	2⅛	2½	3	3¼	3½	4
Nails per lb.	Common	870	543	294	254	167		101	66	61	47	29
	Box	635	473	406	236	210	145	94	88	71	39	
	Cement-coated			527	387	293	223	153	111	81	64	52
	Finish	1350	880	630	535	288		196	124	113	93	39
	Masonry			155	138	100	78	64	48	43	34	

SCREWS & OTHER HARDWARE

The advent of the screw gun and numerous types of driver bits for drills have made screws a mainstay of the carpentry trade. With literally hundreds of different screws and types of fastening hardware available, there is a specific screw for almost every job. But, for most carpentry jobs you will only need to consider a few general-purpose types. Although nails are still preferred for framing jobs, screws have replaced nails for hanging drywall, installing blocking between studs, and attaching sheathing and flooring. Screws are also used to attach a workpiece to plaster, brick, or concrete, which requires an anchoring device (opposite page, top).

Screws are categorized according to length, slot style, head shape, and gauge. The thickness of the screw body is indicated by the gauge number. The larger the number, the larger the screw. Large screws provide extra holding power; small screws are less likely to split a workpiece. There are various styles of screw slot, including Phillips, slotted, and square. Square-drive screwdrivers are increasing in popularity because they grip the screw head tightly, but Phillips head screws are still the most popular.

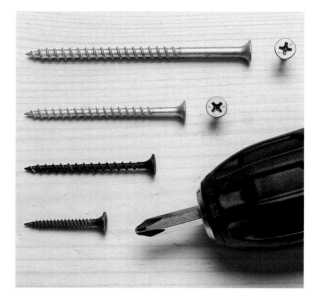

Most screws are now designed to be driven with a power screwdriver. They don't require pilot holes in soft wood, and the bugle-shaped heads allow the screws to countersink themselves. Use drywall screws for general-purpose, convenient fastening indoors. Deck screws are corrosion-resistant screws made specifically for outdoor use. Use deck screws with the correct coating for the lumber being used.

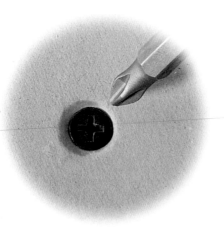

Easily recognizable by their bugle-shaped heads, drywall screws are designed to dimple the surface of the drywall without ripping the facing paper.

Use protector plates where wires or pipes pass through framing members and are less than 1¼" from the edge. The plates prevent drywall screws or nails from puncturing wires or pipes.

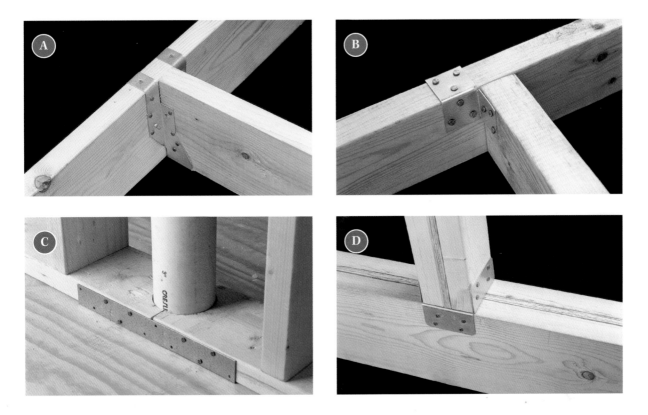

Metal framing connectors may be required in some communities, especially in areas prone to high winds or earthquakes. Metal joist hangers (A), stud ties (B), connector straps (C), and post-and-beam saddles (D) all provide extra reinforcement to structural joints. Wood joints made with metal connectors are stronger than toenailed joints. Metal connectors must be installed with approved fasteners.

USING MASONRY & WALL ANCHORS

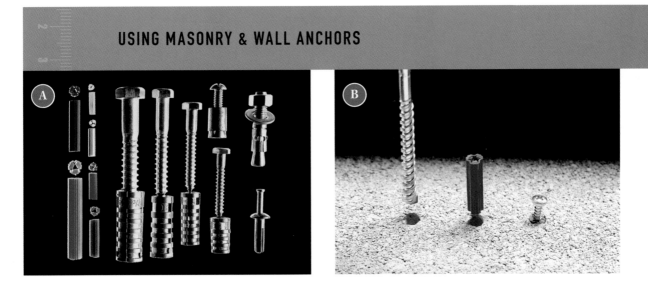

A   Use wall anchors to attach hardware or lumber to plaster, concrete, or brick. Choose an anchor that is equal in length to the thickness of the wall's surface material. Plastic plugs are used for anchoring in hollow walls.

B   To install a wall anchor, drill a pilot hole equal in diameter to the plastic anchor. Insert the anchor in the hole and drive it flush with the wall surface. Insert the screw and tighten it; as the anchor expands, it will create a tight grip.

GLUES & ADHESIVES

When used properly, glues and adhesives can be stronger than the materials they hold together. Use hot glue in lightweight woodworking projects, carpenter's glue for wood joints, and carpentry adhesive for preliminary installation of thin panels and lumber. Panel adhesive, a thinner formula that can be applied from a tube or with a brush, is used to install paneling, wainscoting, and other lightweight tongue-and-groove materials. Masonry adhesive is used for securing top courses of interlocking blocks.

Caulks are designed to permanently close joints, fill gaps in woodwork, and hide subtle imperfections.

Different caulks are made of different compounds and vary greatly in durability and workability. Most caulk is applied with a caulk gun, but some types are available in squeeze tubes for smaller applications. While silicone caulks last longer, many are not paintable and are difficult to smooth out. Latex caulks are less durable than silicone, but are much easier to work with, especially when used to hide gaps. Caulks are available for bond to masonry, glass, tile, metals, wood, fiberglass, and plastic. Read the label carefully to choose the right caulk for the job.

Carpentry adhesives include (clockwise from top right): clear adhesive caulk, for sealing gaps in damp areas; waterproof construction adhesive, for bonding lumber for outdoor projects; multi-purpose adhesive, for attaching paneling and forming strong bonds between lumber pieces; electric hot glue gun and glue sticks, for bonding small decorative trim pieces on built-ins; wood glues and all-purpose glue, for many woodworking projects.

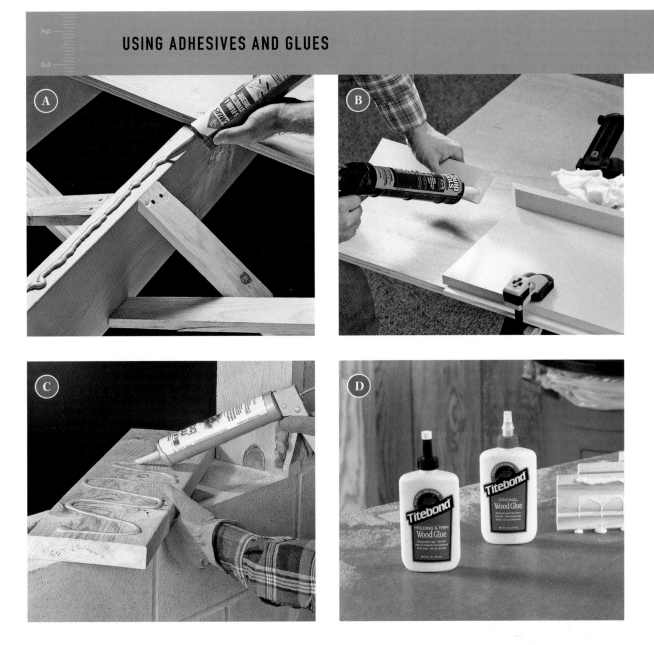

A   Strengthen floors and decks and reduce squeaks with joist and deck adhesive. For outdoor applications, make sure you choose a waterproof adhesive.

B   Construction adhesive adds strength to carpentry and woodworking joints. It also has two advantages over glue. It has high initial tack, so parts don't slide apart, and it retains some flexibility after drying.

C   Exterior-grade construction adhesive fortifies the bond between wood structural members and the masonry house foundation. Additional fasteners, such as powder-actuated nails, are still needed.

D   Specialty molding and trim glue has a thicker formulation than standard wood glue to resist running and dripping on vertical surfaces. It is tackier than regular glue, which helps hold ceiling trims in place when they are positioned, creating a small amount of time for you to fasten them with nails.

ANATOMY
OF A HOUSE

Anatomy Details

Many remodeling projects, like adding new doors or windows, require that you remove one or more studs in a load-bearing wall to create an opening. When planning your project, remember that new openings require a permanent support beam called a header, above the removed studs, to carry the structural load directly.

The required size for the header is set by local building codes and varies according to the width of the rough opening. For a window or door opening, a header can be built from two pieces of 2-inch dimensional lumber sandwiched around ⅜-inch plywood (chart, right).

When a large portion of a load-bearing wall (or an entire wall) is removed, a laminated beam product can be used to make the new header.

Recommended Header Sizes

Rough Opening WIdth	Recommended Header Construction
Up to 3 ft.	⅜" plywood between two 2 × 4s
3 ft. to 5 ft.	⅜" plywood between two 2 × 6s
5 ft. to 7 ft.	⅜" plywood between two 2 × 8s
7 ft. to 8 ft.	⅜" plywood between two 2 × 10s

If you will be removing more than one wall stud, make temporary supports to carry the structural load until the header is installed.

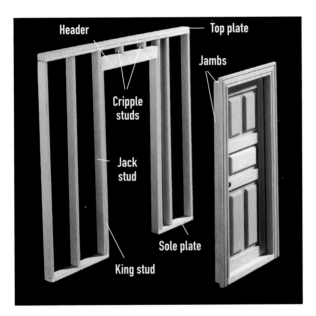

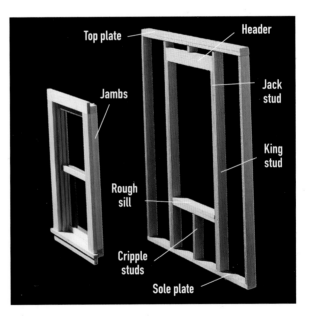

Door opening: The structural load above the door is carried by cripple studs that rest on a header. The ends of the header are supported by jack studs (also known as trimmer studs) and king studs that transfer the load to the sole plate and the foundation of the house. The rough opening for a door should be 1" wider and ½" taller than the dimensions of the door unit, including the jambs. This extra space lets you adjust the door unit during installation.

Window opening: The structural load above the window is carried by cripple studs resting on a header. The ends of the header are supported by jack studs and king studs, which transfer the load to the sole plate and the foundation of the house. The rough sill, which helps anchor the window unit but carries no structural weight, is supported by cripple studs. To provide room for adjustments during installation, the rough opening for a window should be 1" wider and ½" taller than the window unit, including the jambs.

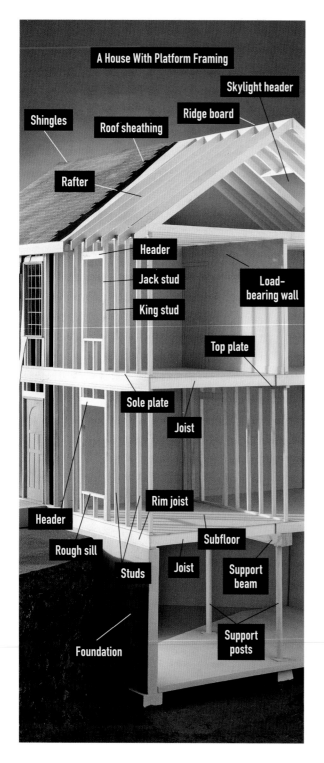

A House With Platform Framing

- Skylight header
- Shingles
- Roof sheathing
- Ridge board
- Rafter
- Header
- Jack stud
- Load-bearing wall
- King stud
- Top plate
- Sole plate
- Joist
- Rim joist
- Header
- Subfloor
- Rough sill
- Studs
- Joist
- Support beam
- Foundation
- Support posts

BEFORE YOU START A do-it-yourself carpentry project, you should familiarize yourself with a few basic elements of home construction and remodeling. Take some time to get comfortable with the terminology of the models shown on the next few pages. The understanding you will gain in this section will make it easier to plan your project, buy the right materials, and clear up any confusion you might have about the internal design of your home.

If your project includes modifying exterior or load-bearing walls, you must determine if your house was built using platform- or balloon-style framing. The framing style of your home determines what kind of temporary supports you will need to install while the work is in progress. If you have trouble determining what type of framing was used

Platform Framing

Platform framing (photos, above and left) is identified by the floor-level sole plates and ceiling-level top plates to which the wall studs are attached. Most houses built after 1930 use platform framing. If you do not have access to unfinished areas, you can remove the wall surface at the bottom of a wall to determine what kind of framing was used in your home.

in your home, refer to the original blueprints, if you have them, or consult a building contractor or licensed home inspector.

Framing in a new door or window on an exterior wall normally requires installing a header. Make sure that the header you install meets the requirements of your local building code, and always install cripple studs where necessary.

Floors and ceilings consist of sheet materials, joists, and support beams. All floors used as living areas must have joists with at least 2 × 8 construction.

There are two types of walls: load-bearing and partition. Load-bearing walls require temporary supports during wall removal or framing of a door or window. Partition walls carry no structural load and do not require temporary supports.

Balloon Framing

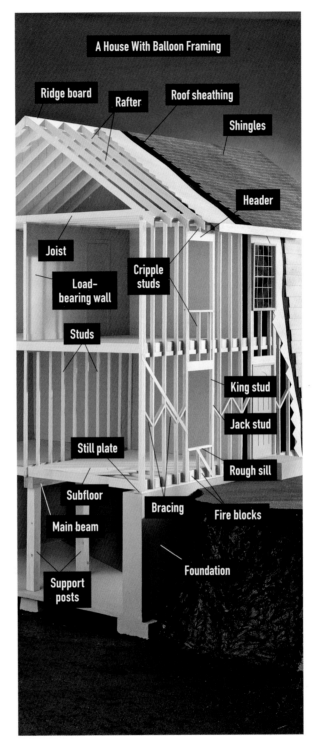

A House With Balloon Framing

Ridge board · Rafter · Roof sheathing · Shingles · Header · Joist · Cripple studs · Load-bearing wall · Studs · King stud · Jack stud · Still plate · Rough sill · Subfloor · Bracing · Fire blocks · Main beam · Foundation · Support posts

Balloon framing (photos, right and above) is identified by wall studs that run uninterrupted from the roof to a sill plate on the foundation, without the sole plates and top plates found in platform-framed walls (page 88). Balloon framing was used in houses built before 1930, and it is still used in some new home styles, especially those with high vaulted ceilings.

Framing Options for Window & Door Openings (new lumber shown in yellow)

Using an existing opening avoids the need for new framing. This is a good option in homes with masonry exteriors, which are difficult to alter. Order a replacement unit that is 1" narrower and ½" shorter than the rough opening.

Framing a new opening is the only solution when you're installing a window or door where none existed or when you're replacing a unit with one that is much larger.

Enlarging an existing opening simplifies the framing. In many cases, you can use an existing king stud and jack stud to form one side of the new opening.

Wall Anatomy

Load-bearing walls carry the structural weight of your home. In platform-framed houses, load-bearing walls can be identified by double top plates made from two layers of framing lumber. Load-bearing walls include all exterior walls and any interior walls that are aligned above support beams.

Partition walls are interior walls that do not carry the structural weight of the house. They have a single top plate and can be perpendicular to the floor and ceiling joists but are not aligned above support beams. Any interior wall that is parallel to floor and ceiling joists is a partition wall.

Floor & Ceiling Anatomy

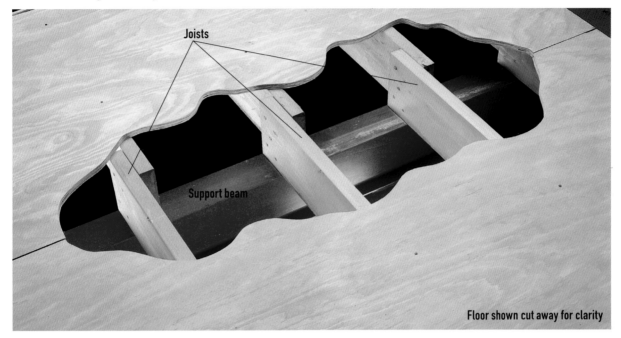

Joists

Support beam

Floor shown cut away for clarity

Joists carry the structural load of floors and ceilings. The ends of the joists rest on support beams, foundations, or load-bearing walls. Rooms used as living areas must be supported by floor joists that are at least 2 × 8 in size. Floors with smaller joists can be reinforced with sister joists.

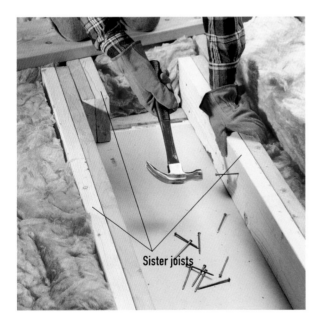

Sister joists

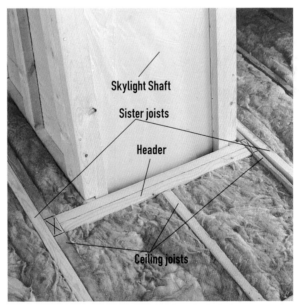

Skylight Shaft

Sister joists

Header

Ceiling joists

Floors with 2 × 6 joists, like those sometimes found in attics, cannot support living areas unless a sister joist is attached alongside each original joist to strengthen it. This often is necessary when an attic is converted to a living area.

Sister joists also are used to help support a header when ceiling joists must be cut, such as when framing a skylight shaft.

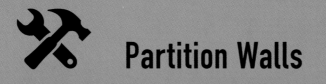

Partition Walls

Wall studs

Top plate

Cripple stud

Header

Jack stud

King stud

Sole plate

Tools & Materials

Protective eyewear
Chalk line
Circular saw
Framing square
Plumb bob
Powder-actuated nailer
T-bevel
2 x 4 lumber
Blocking lumber
16d and 8d common nails
Concrete fasteners
Drywall screws

A typical partition wall consists of top and bottom plates and 2 × 4 studs spaced 16" on-center. Use 2 × 6 lumber for walls that will hold large plumbing pipes (inset).

PARTITION WALLS ARE non-load-bearing walls typically built with 2 × 4 lumber, but they can also be built with 3⅝-inch steel studs. Walls holding plumbing pipes can be framed with 2 × 6 lumber. On a concrete floor, use pressure-treated lumber for the bottom plates.

This project involves building a wall in place, rather than framing a complete wall on the floor and tilting it upright, as in new construction. The build-in-place method allows for variations in floor and ceiling levels and is generally much easier for remodeling projects.

If your wall will include a door or other opening, see pages 94 to 99. Check the local building codes for requirements about fireblocking in partition walls. And after your walls are framed and the mechanical rough-ins are completed, install metal protector plates where pipes and wires run through framing members.

Nail guns will help improve your nailing accuracy. You'll never need to worry about a glanced hammer blow denting the wood or bending a nail. Air nailers never miss the nail head. As long as you choose the correct nails for the application and set the air compressor pressure properly, a pneumatic nailer will drive and set nails reliably, time after time.

VARIATIONS FOR FASTENING TOP PLATES TO JOISTS

When a new wall is perpendicular to the ceiling or floor joists above, attach the top plate directly to the joists, using 16d nails.

When a new wall falls between parallel joists, install 2 × 4 blocking between the joists every 24". If the new wall is aligned with a parallel joist, install blocks on both sides of the wall, and attach the top plate to the joist (inset).

VARIATIONS FOR FASTENING BOTTOM PLATES TO JOISTS

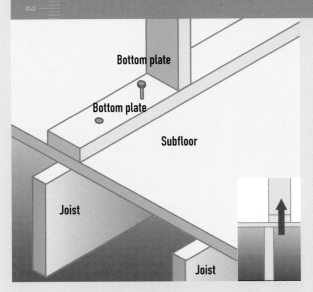

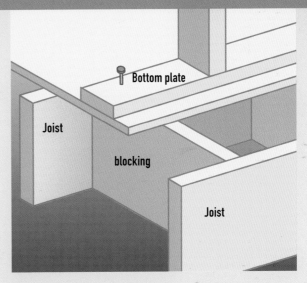

If a new wall is aligned with a joist below, install the bottom plate directly over the joist or off-center over the joist (inset). Off-center placement allows you to nail into the joist but provides room underneath the plate for pipes or wiring to go up into the wall.

If a new wall falls between parallel joists, install 2 × 6 or larger blocking between the two joists below, spaced 24" on center. Nail the bottom plate through the subfloor and into the blocking.

1   Mark the location of the leading edge of the new wall's top plate, then snap a chalk line through the marks across the joists or blocks. Use a framing square, or take measurements, to make sure the line is perpendicular to any intersecting walls. Cut the top and bottom plates to length.

2   Set the plates together with their ends flush. Measure from the end of one plate, and make marks for the location of each stud. The first stud should fall 15 ¼" from the end; every stud thereafter should fall 16" on center. Thus, the first 4 × 8-ft. drywall panel will cover the first stud and "break" in the center of the fourth stud. Use a square to extend the marks across both plates. Draw an X at each stud location.

3   Position the top plate against the joists, aligning its leading edge with the chalk line. Attach the plate with two 16d nails driven into each joist. Start at one end, and adjust the plate as you go to keep the leading edge flush with the chalk line.

4   To position the bottom plate, hang a plumb bob from the side edge of the top plate so the point nearly touches the floor. When it hangs motionless, mark the point's location on the floor. Make plumb markings at each end of the top plate, then snap a chalk line between the marks. Position the bottom plate along the chalk line, and use the plumb bob to align the stud markings between the two plates.

5   Fasten the bottom plate to the floor. On concrete, use a powder-actuated nailer or masonry screws, driving a pin or screw every 16". On wood floors, use 16d nails driven into the joists below.

6   Measure between the plates for the length of each stud. Cut each stud so it fits snugly in place but is not so tight that it bows the joists above. If you cut a stud too short, see if it will fit somewhere else down the wall.

7   Install the studs by toenailing them at a 60° angle through the sides of the studs and into the plates. At each end, drive two 8d nails through one side of the stud and one more through the center on the other side.

Framing Corners (shown in cutaways)

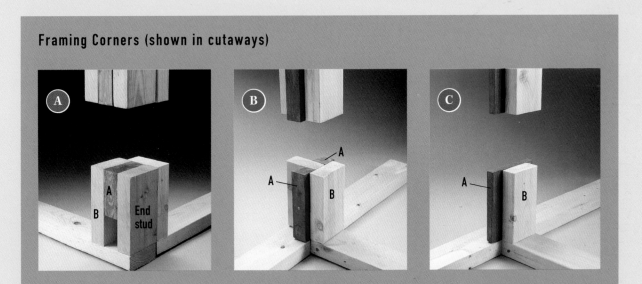

A   L-corners: Nail 2 × 4 spacers (A) to the inside of the end stud. Nail an extra stud (B) to the spacers. The extra stud provides a surface to attach drywall at the inside corner.

B   T-corner meets stud: Fasten 2 × 2 backers (A) to each side of the side-wall stud (B). The backers provide a nailing surface for drywall.

C   T-corner between studs: Fasten a 1 × 6 backer (A) to the end stud (B) with drywall screws. The backer provides a nailing surface for drywall.

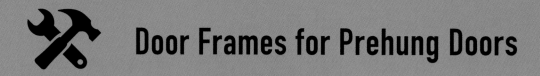

Door Frames for Prehung Doors

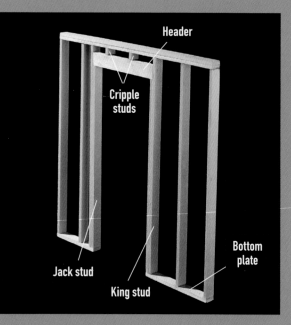

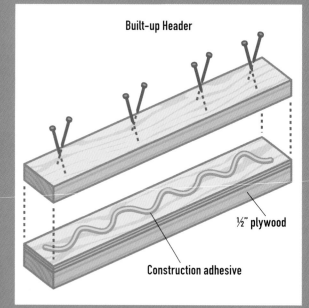

Built-up Header

½" plywood

Construction adhesive

Door frames for prehung doors start with king studs that attach to the top and bottom plates. Inside the king studs, jack studs support the header at the top of the opening. Cripple studs continue the wall-stud layout above the opening. The dimensions of the framed opening are referred to as the rough opening.

In non-load-bearing walls, the header may be a 2 × 4 laid flat. A built-up header is constructed of two 2× pieces of lumber glued and screwed around a piece of ½" plywood.

FRAMING FOR PREHUNG DOORS

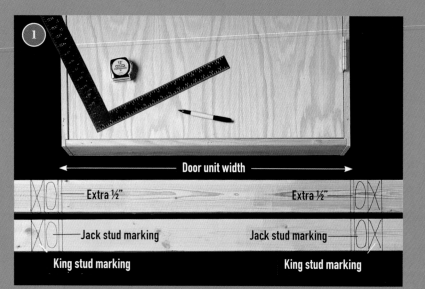

Door unit width

Extra ½"   Extra ½"

Jack stud marking   Jack stud marking

King stud marking   King stud marking

1   To mark the layout for the door frame, measure the width of the door unit along the bottom. Add 1" to this dimension to determine the width of the rough opening (the distance between the jack studs). This gives you a ½" gap on each side for adjusting the door frame during installation. Mark the top and bottom plates for the jack and king studs.

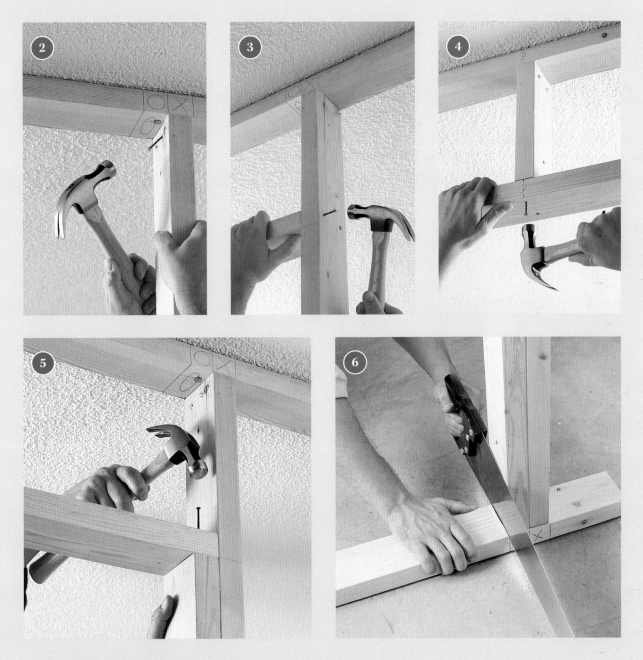

2 After you've installed the wall plates (see page 92), cut the king studs and toenail them in place at the appropriate markings.

3 Measure the full length of the door unit, then add ½" to determine the height of the rough opening. Using that dimension, measure up from the floor and mark the king studs. Cut a 2 × 4 header to fit between the king studs. Position the header flat, with its bottom face at the marks, and secure it to the king studs with 16d nails.

4 Cut and install a cripple stud above the header, centered between the king studs. Install any additional cripples required to maintain the 16" on-center layout of the standard studs in the rest of the wall.

5 Cut the jack studs to fit snugly under the header. Fasten them in place by nailing down through the header, then drive 10d nails through the faces of the jack studs and into the king studs, spaced 16" apart.

6 Saw through the bottom plate so it's flush with the inside faces of the jack studs. Remove the cut-out portion of the plate. If you're finishing the wall with drywall, hang the door after the drywall is installed.

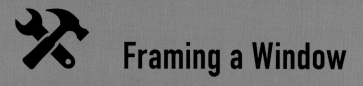

Framing a Window

Tools & Materials

Tape measure
Pencil
Combination square
Hammer
Level
Circular saw
Handsaw
Pry bar
Nippers
Drill
Reciprocating saw
Stapler
Nail set
Caulk gun
10d common nails
5d galvanized roofing nails
Shims
2× lumber
⅛" plywood
Building paper
Drip edge
10d galvanized casing nails
8d casing nails
Fiberglass insulation
Paintable silicone caulk

MANY WINDOWS MUST be custom-ordered several weeks in advance. To save time, you can complete the interior framing before the window unit arrives, but be sure you have the exact dimensions of the window unit before building the frame. Do not remove the outside wall surface until you have the window and accessories and are ready to install them.

Follow the manufacturer's specifications for the rough opening size when framing for a window. The listed opening usually is 1-inch wider and ½-inch taller than the actual dimensions of the window unit. The following pages show techniques for woodframe houses with platform framing.

If your house has balloon framing (built before the 1930s) consult a professional.

If your house has masonry walls or if you are installing polymer-coated windows, you may want to attach your window using masonry clips instead of nails.

Tip

Most garages don't have windows—partly for security and partly because of the expense. This is a great project for adding windows to a garage to allow natural light into your work space while building your carpentry skills.

FRAMING A WINDOW OPENING

1   Prepare the project site and remove the interior wall surfaces. Measure and mark the rough opening width on the sole plate. Mark the locations of the jack studs and king studs on the sole plate. Where practical, use the existing studs as king studs.

2   Measure and cut the king studs, as needed, to fit between the sole plate and the top plate. Position the king studs and toenail them to the sole plate with 10d nails.

3   Check the king studs with a level to make sure they are plumb, then toenail them to the top plate with 10d nails.

4   Measuring from the floor, mark the top of the rough opening on one of the king studs. This line represents the bottom of the window header. For most windows, the recommended rough opening is ½" taller than the height of the window frame.

continued

5   Measure and mark where the top of the window header will fit against the king stud. The header size depends on the distance between the king studs. Use a carpenter's level to extend the lines across the old studs to the opposite king stud.

6   Measure down from header line and mark the double rough sill on the king stud. Use a carpenter's level to extend the lines across the old studs to the opposite king stud. Make temporary supports (page xx) if removing more than one stud.

7   Set a circular saw to its maximum blade depth, then cut through the old studs along the lines marking the bottom of the rough sill and along the lines marking the top of the header. Do not cut the king studs. On each stud, make an additional cut about 3" above the sill cut. Finish the cuts with a handsaw.

8   Knock out the 3" stud sections, then tear out the old studs inside the rough opening, using a pry bar. Clip away any exposed nails, using nippers. The remaining sections of the cut studs will serve as cripple studs for the window.

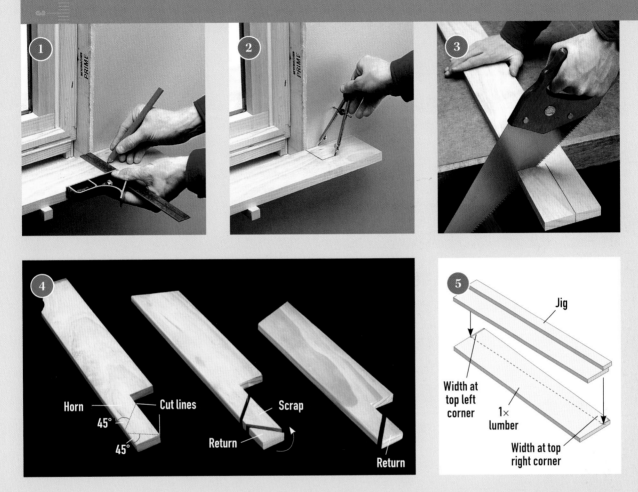

Horn | Cut lines | 45° | 45° | Return | Scrap | Return

Jig | Width at top left corner | 1× lumber | Width at top right corner

1   Cut the stool to length, with several inches at each end for creating the horn returns. With the stool centered at the window and tight against the drywall, shim it to its finished height. At each corner, measure the distance between the window frame and the stool, then mark that dimension on the stool.

2   Open a compass so it touches the wall and the tip of the rough opening mark on the stool, then scribe the plane of the wall onto the stool to complete the cutting line for the horn.

3   Cut out the notches for the horn, using a jigsaw or a sharp handsaw. Test-fit the stool, making any minor adjustments with a plane or a rasp to fit it tightly to the window and the walls.

4   To create a return at the horn of the stool, miter-cut the return pieces at 45° angles. Mark the stool at its overall length and cut it to size with 45° miter cuts. Glue the return to the mitered end of the horn so the grain wraps around the corner. Note: Use this same technique to create the returns on the apron (step 13), but make the cuts with the apron held on edge, rather than flat.

5   Where extensions are needed, cut the head extension to its finished length—the distance between the window side jambs plus the thickness of both side extensions (typically 1× stock). For the width, measure the distance between the window jamb and the finished wall at each corner, then mark the measurements on the ends of the extension. Use a straightedge to draw a reference line connecting the points. Build a simple cutting jig, as shown.

continued

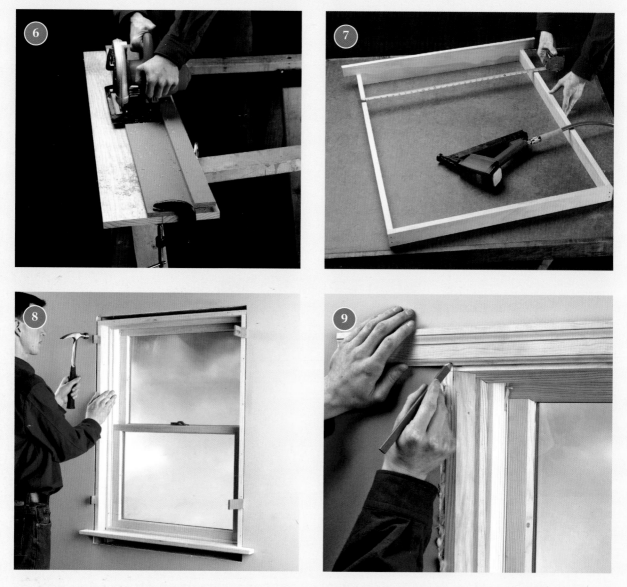

6   Clamp the jig on the reference line, then rip the extension to width using a circular saw; keep the baseplate tight against the jig and move the saw smoothly along the cut. Reposition the clamp when you near the end of the cut. Cut both side extensions to length and width, using the same technique as for the head extension (step 5).

7   Build a box frame with the extensions and stool, using 6d finish nails and a pneumatic nailer. Measure to make sure the box has the same dimensions as the window jambs. Drive nails through the top of the head extension into the side extensions and through the bottom of the stool into side extensions.

8   Apply wood glue to the back edge of the frame, then position it against the front edge of the window jambs. Use wood shims to adjust the frame, making sure pieces are flush with window jambs. Fasten the frame at each shim location, using 8d finish nails driven through pilot holes. Loosely pack insulation between framing members and extensions.

9   On the edge of each extension, mark a ¼" reveal at the corners, the middle, and the stool. Place a length of casing along the head extension, aligned with the reveal marks at the corners. Mark where the reveal marks intersect, then make 45° miter cuts at each point. Reposition the casing at the head extension, and attach using 4d finish nails at the extensions and 6d finish nails at the framing members.

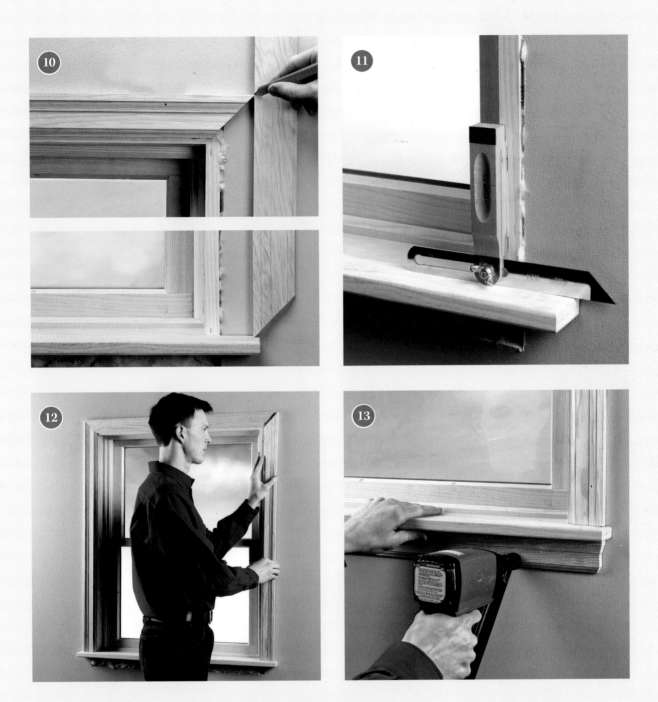

10 Cut the side casings to rough length, leaving the ends slightly long for final trimming. Miter one end at 45°.
    With the pointed end on the stool, mark the height of the side casing at the top edge of the head casing.

11 To get a tight fit for side casings, align one side of a T-bevel with the reveal, mark the side extension, and position the other
    side flush against the horn. Transfer the angle from the T-bevel to the end of the casing, and cut the casing to length.

12 Test-fit the casings, making any final adjustments with a plane or rasp. Fasten the casing with 4d finish nails at the
    extensions and 6d finish nails at the framing members.

13 Cut the apron to length, leaving a few inches at each end for creating the returns (step 4). Position the apron tight
    against the bottom edge of the stool, then attach it using 6d finish nails driven every 12".

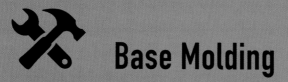

Base Molding

BASEBOARD TRIM IS INSTALLED TO CONCEAL

the joint between the finished floor and the wallcovering. It also serves to protect the drywall at the floor. Installing plain, one-piece baseboard such as ranch-style base or cove base is a straightforward project. Outside corner joints are mitered, inside corners are coped, and long runs are joined with scarf cuts.

The biggest difficulty to installing base is dealing with out-of-plumb and nonsquare corners. However, a T-bevel makes these obstacles easy to overcome.

Plan the order of your installation prior to cutting any pieces and lay out a specific piece for each length of wall. It may be helpful to mark the type of cut on the back of each piece so you don't have any confusion during the install.

Locate all studs and mark them with painter's tape 6 inches higher than your molding height. If you need to make any scarf joints along a wall, make sure they fall on the center of a stud. Before you begin nailing trim in place, take the time to pre-finish the moldings. Doing so will minimize the cleanup afterward.

Tools & Materials
Pencil
Tape measure
Power miter saw
T-bevel
Coping saw
Metal file set
Pneumatic finish nail gun & compressor
Moldings
Pneumatic fasteners
Carpenter's glue
Finishing putty

INSTALLING ONE-PIECE BASE MOLDING

1. Measure, cut, and install the first piece of baseboard. Butt both ends into the corners tightly. For longer lengths, it is a good idea to cut the piece slightly oversized (up to $\frac{1}{16}$" on strips over 10 ft. long) and "spring" it into place. Nail the molding in place with two nails at every stud location.

2. Cut the second piece of molding oversized by 6" to 10" and cope-cut the adjoining end to the first piece. Fine-tune the cope with a metal file and sandpaper. Dry-fit the joint, adjusting it as necessary to produce a tight-fitting joint.

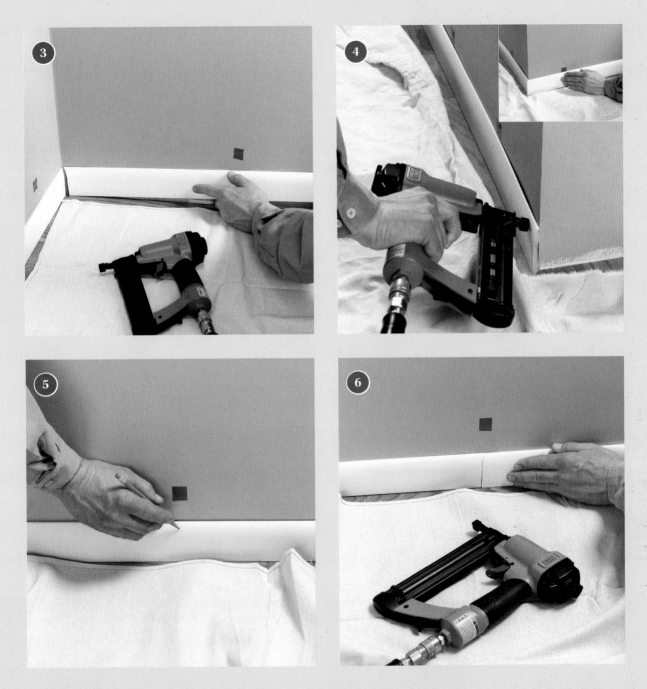

3   Check the corner for square with a framing square. If necessary, adjust the miter cut of your saw. Use a T-bevel to transfer the proper angle. Cut the second piece (coped) to length and install it with two nails at each stud location.

4   Adjust the miter angle of your saw to cut the adjoining outside corner piece (3). Test-fit the cut to ensure a tight joint (inset photo). Remove the mating piece of trim and fasten the first piece for the outside corner joint.

5   Lay out any scarf joints by placing the piece in position so that the previous joint is tight and then marking the center of a stud location nearest the opposite end. Set the angle of your saw to a 30° angle and cut the molding at the marked location.

6   Nail the third piece in place, making sure the outside corner joint is tight. Cut the end of the fourth piece to match the scarf joint angle and nail it in place with two nails at each stud location. Add the remaining pieces of molding, fill the nail holes with putty, and apply a final coat of finish.

WORKSHOPS

ONCE YOU BEGIN to acquire tools and materials for carpentry projects, you will find that organization is a must. Lumber and sheet goods are bulky, and you will probably have leftover pieces that you want to keep—but where? This section gives you pointers on where and how.

Using pegboard is a classic way of organizing that still works great as an infinitely adjustable storage system. Nicely framed pegboard will enhance any shop space.

Work surfaces are also important. A pair of heavy duty sawhorses and a piece of plywood make a great temporary table. Directions for building the sawhorses are included, and are a good practice project for developing your new carpentry skills.

A sturdy workbench, if you have the room, is a complement to any garage or basement. Plans for a sturdy, durable, and simple to build workbench are included.

STORAGE STRATEGIES

Your stored tools and supplies should be well organized, easy to access, and out of the way. This is the best way to ensure your work surfaces are clean and ready for the next phase of a project. Depending on the type of work you do, you'll probably need plenty of open space to facilitate large projects as needed, or to temporarily reconfigure the shop to accommodate materials that need to be cut down to a manageable size, etc. If this requires the use of shared spaces—for example, making room in the garage by pulling the car into the driveway—it helps to have tools and work surfaces that are easily moved or can be set up and knocked down quickly.

Here are some of the key strategies that help make an integrated shop work with its surroundings:

For storage, think volume, not just floor space. Shelving units that rise from floor to ceiling make better use of floor space than shelves that stop at a convenient, reachable height. The upper shelves can be filled with seldom-used items. Also look for opportunities where overhead storage can help keep the floor area and work surfaces clear. Open stud cavities in an unfinished garage or utility room offer free space for small shelves or long, thin material stored on end.

For work that involves multiple stages or tool operations, plan for mobility and adaptability. Work benches, materials racks, and even large stationary tools can be outfitted with heavy-duty locking casters so you can roll them out when you need them and roll them back when you're done. You can build your own caster bases or shop around for compatible manufactured versions. Some power tools are designed for use with specific portable bases or come with their own folding stands, so check with the manufacturers of your tools.

Plan workstations for double duty: a permanent bench or work table is already taking up floor space, so why not use the space above and below for storage? For example, a lumber rack above a saw table makes it easy to grab stock as you go. Rolling carts or pull-out bins and drawers beneath a bench can hold other tools plus blades or bits for the station's main tool. Small woodworking shops can save space by combining a saw table or extension wing with a router table.

Consider using outdoor spaces for work and storage. Rolling tool bases and portable workstations simplify setup outdoors. Cutting sheet goods (especially MDF and particleboard) outdoors helps keep dust down in garage shops and simplifies transport of materials into basement workspaces. A simple lean-to shed built against the back wall of the house or garage is a great way to keep materials out of the elements and out of the way. A permanent outdoor workbench made with weather-resistant materials is handy for rough-cutting materials or finishing projects in nice weather. Here are some other tips for saving space in a small shop:

- Cover garage or basement walls with plywood for hanging tools, bins, or cabinets wherever you need them. Paint the plywood a light color for better light reflection.
- Store lumber, sheet goods, and other large materials on a rolling cart or rack for easy access and to facilitate unloading and transport from your vehicle.
- Build custom cubbies or shelving for storing frequently used equipment, like portable power tools, without their bulky cases. Incorporate tote-away boxes or sliding trays for blades, bits, and accessories.
- Keep a trash barrel or bin underneath one or both ends of workstations for discarding scrap material as you work.
- In a basement shop, store clamps and similar devices by clamping them to the floor joists above (secure bar clamps to only one joist; clamping across joists can pull them together, thus releasing other clamps)
- For a lightweight, portable work table, use a hollow-core door finished with polyurethane (or other varnish) laid over foldup metal sawhorses.

A utility shop. This compact shop area was made with inexpensive utility cabinets and a plywood work top.

You can build this space-saving lumber rack with a few 2 × 4 studs and some steel pipe: drill matching holes in all of the studs, then fasten one to the side of every other garage-wall stud. Add a plywood shelf or two for storing small pieces. Don't use garage wall studs as the pipe supports; the holes would weaken the studs too much.

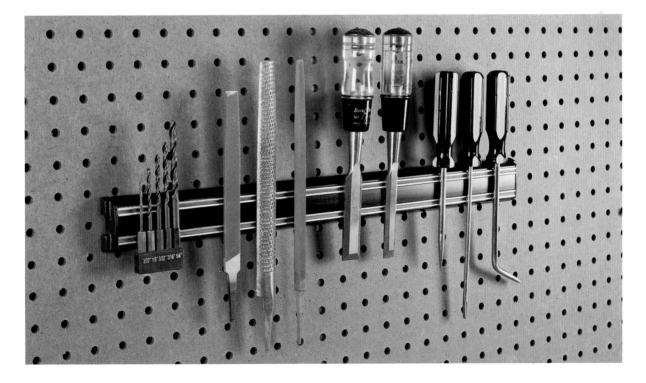

Magnetic bar strips, typically used for holding knives in the kitchen, are just as handy for storing chisels, files, awls, and other metal tools in the workshop.

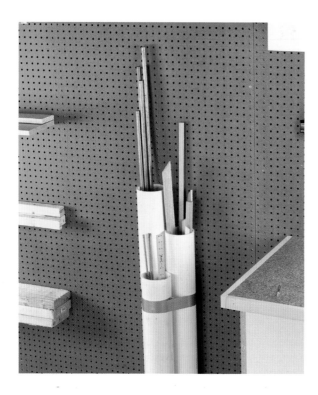

Lengths of plastic plumbing pipe or cardboard carpet-roll tubes make a safe and handy home for dowels, rods, and fine trim pieces. Gang the cylinders together with strapping or duct tape to create a freestanding storage unit.

Build a Bench Buddy. Create more storage space by attaching pieces of pegboard to the sides of the workbench with drywall screws and finish washers.

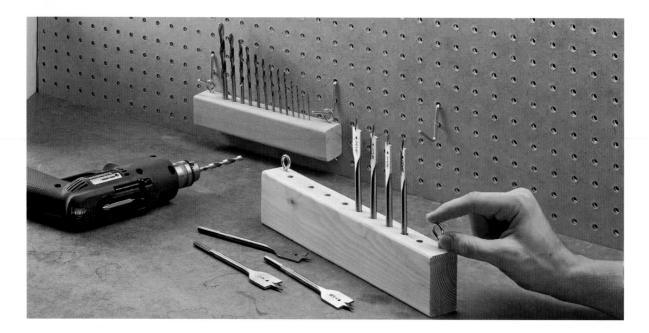

Metal drill and router bits have finely honed cutting edges that can be ruined if the bits bump against each other inside a toolbox or workbench drawer. To protect tool bits from damage, make a storage block by boring holes in a scrap piece of lumber. Attach screw eyes to the top of the block so it can be stored on pegboard hooks and taken down when a bit is needed.

Add storage space in an unfinished utility area by covering the studs with panels of pegboard. These panels are ideal for storing drywall framing squares, levels, garden tools, and other large items.

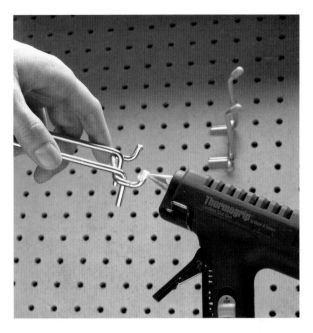

Pegboard hooks frequently fall out when an item is removed. End this aggravating problem by gluing the hooks to the pegboard with a hot glue gun. If you need to reposition the pegboard hooks, heat them for a few seconds with a heat gun until the glue softens.

Store long materials in the space between open ceiling joists in an unfinished utility area. Attach ¾" plywood furring strips across the joists with 2½" drywall screws or lag screws. Space the strips no more than 36" apart to provide adequate support. Make sure to avoid any electrical cables or fixtures located between the ceiling joists. Some homeowners attach boards across the bottom of the ceiling joists to make out-of-the-way storage shelves for small cans and other shop items.

Skillbuilder

Use leftover pieces of plywood or 1" lumber to build sturdy storage boxes for heavy hardware. Assemble the boxes with 1¼" drywall screws and glue. Try to build each box the exact same size. Organize the storage boxes on utility shelves for easy access. If you wish, attach metal handles to the boxes.

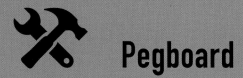 # Pegboard

Tools & Materials

Work gloves
Eye protection
Tape measure
Level
Circular saw or jigsaw
Drill with bits
Stud finder
Clamps
1 × 2" furring strips
Caulk gun
Drywall screws (1", 2½")
Panel adhesive
Picture frame molding (optional)
Paint roller
Varnish or primer and paint
Pegboard

Pegboard systems are classic storage solutions for garages and other utility areas. Outfitted with a variety of hangers, they offer flexibility and convenience when used to store hand tools and other small shop items.

PEGBOARD, ALSO CALLED perforated hardboard or perfboard, is one of the simplest and least expensive storage solutions for hanging tools and other lightweight objects. When mounted to the wall and outfitted with metal hooks, pegboard provides a convenient way to keep items from getting lost in the back of a drawer or the bottom of a tool chest. Pegboard also makes it easy to change the arrangement or collection of your wall-hung items, because you can reposition the metal hooks any way you like without measuring, drilling holes, or hammering nails into the wall. In fact, pegboard has served as a low-cost storage option for so long that there are a multitude of different hooks and brackets you can buy to accommodate nearly anything you want to hang. Any home center will carry both the pegboard and the hooks.

You need to install pegboard correctly to get the most value from it. If your garage walls have exposed studs, you can simply screw pegboard to the studs. The empty bays between the studs will provide the necessary clearance for inserting the hooks. On a finished wall, however, you'll need to install a framework of furring strips behind the pegboard to create the necessary clearance and provide some added stiffness. It's also a good idea to build a frame around your pegboard to give the project a neat, finished appearance.

If your garage tends to be damp, seal both faces of the pegboard with several coats of varnish or primer and exterior paint; otherwise it will absorb moisture and swell up or even delaminate.

PEGBOARD & HANGER HARDWARE STYLES

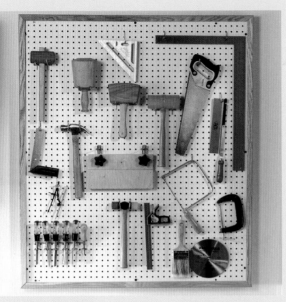

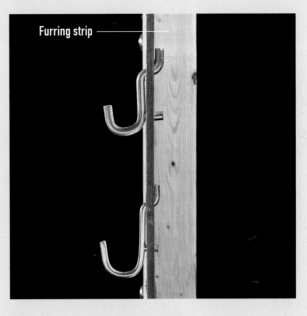

Hanger hardware comes in many shapes and sizes, from the basic J for hanging a single tool to double-prong hangers for hammers and even shelf standards. You can buy assorted hangers in kits or stock up on the type you're likely to use the most.

Two common thicknesses for pegboard hangers are ⅛"-dia. and ³⁄₁₆"-dia., both of which fit into standard pegboard hole configurations. The thicker the hanger, the more it can handle. Both types rely on the mechanical connection with the pegboard and can fail if the holes in the board become elongated. The pegboard must have furring strips on the back side to create a recess for the hangers.

Pegboard is a single-purpose sheet good material. It is used to create a wall surface with storage functionality (occasionally it may be used as a cabinet back where ventilation is desired). Although it comes in ⅛"-thick panels, avoid them in favor of ¼" thick material. Most larger home centers carry it unfinished and in prefinished white. Wood grain and other decorative panels can be found, and you can also buy metal pegboard panels. The standard size holes are ¼" dia. and spaced in a 1" on center grid.

Option

Make a frame from picture frame molding and wrap it around the pegboard to conceal the edge grain and the furring strips. If you can't find picture frame molding with the correct dimensions, mill your own molding by cutting a ⅜"-wide by 1"-deep rabbet into one face of 1 × 2 stock.

1   Cut your pegboard panel to size if you are not install-ing a full sheet (most building centers sell 2 × 4 ft. and 4 × 4 ft. panels in addition to the standard 4 × 8 ft.) If you are cutting with a circular saw, orient the panel face up to prevent tearout on the higher-grade face. If cutting with a jigsaw, the good face of the panel should be down. If possible, plan your cuts so there is an even amount of distance from the holes to all edges.

2   Cut 1 × 2 furring strips to make a frame that is attached to the back side of the pegboard panel. The outside edges of the furring strips should be flush with the edges of the pegboard. Because they will be visible, cut the frame parts so the two side edge strips run the full height of the panel (36" here). Cut a couple of filler strips to fill in between the top and bottom rails.

3   Attach the furring strips to the back of the panel using 1" drywall screws and panel adhesive. Drive the screws through countersunk pilot holes in the panel face. Do not drive screws through the predrilled pegboard holes. Use intermediate furring strips to fill in between the top and bottom. These may be fastened with panel adhesive alone.

4   Paint or top coat the pegboard. You can leave the pegboard unfinished, if you prefer, but a coat of paint or varnish protects the composite material from nicks and dings and hardens it around the hole openings so the holes are less likely to become elongated. A paint roller and short-nap sleeve make quick work of the job.

5   Locate and mark wall studs if your garage wall has a wall covering. Make sure the marks extend above and below the pegboard location so you can see them once the pegboard is positioned on the wall.

6   Tack the pegboard and frame to the wall in the desired location. Drive one 2½" screw partway through the top frame at the center of the pegboard. Place a long level on the top of the pegboard and adjust it to level using the screw as a pivot point.

7   Drive a drywall screw through the top and bottom frame rails at each wall stud location. Drill countersunk pilot holes first. Double-check for level after driving the first screw. Insert hangers as desired.

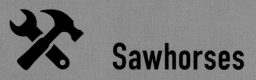

Sawhorses

Tools & Materials (for one sawhorse)

Circular saw
Tape measure
Screw gun or cordless screwdriver
(4) 8-ft. 2 × 4s
2½" drywall screws
(2) Vertical braces, 15 ½"
(2) Top rails, 48"
(1) Bottom brace, 48"
(2) Horizontal braces, 11 ¼"
(4) Legs, 26"

SAWHORSES PROVIDE a stable work surface to support materials during marking and cutting. They can also form the base for temporary scaffolding to use while installing drywall or ceiling panels. A wide top is best for supporting large loads. Small breakdown sawhorses are a good choice if storage space is limited.

For scaffolding, place straight 2 × 10s or 2 × 12s across a pair of heavy-duty sawhorses.

Easy-storing Sawhorse Options

Light-duty metal sawhorses can be folded and hung on the workshop wall when they are not in use.

Buy brackets made from fiberglass or metal, and cut a 48" top rail and four 26" legs from 2 × 4s. Disassemble sawhorses for storage.

BUILDING A HEAVY-DUTY SAWHORSE

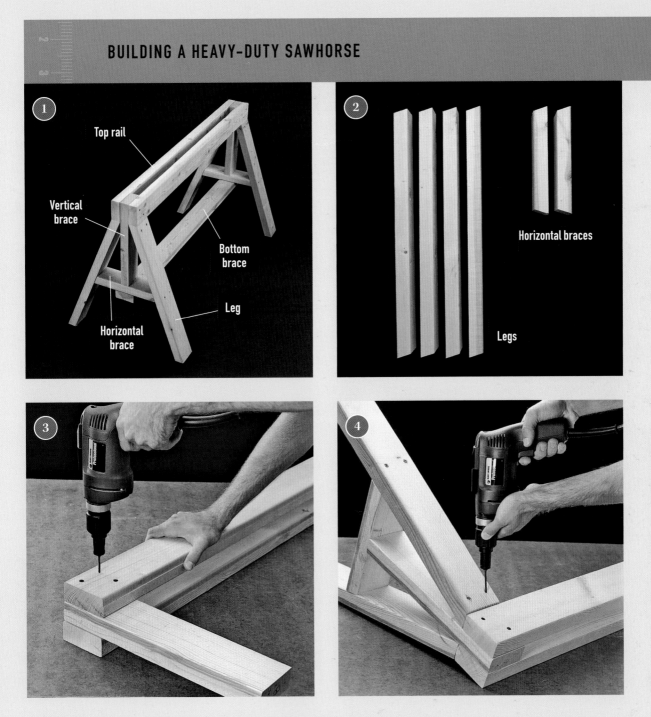

1.   Measure and cut the vertical braces, top rails, and bottom brace to the lengths specified in the Material List (opposite page) using a tape measure and a circular saw.

2.   Set a circular or miter saw to a 17° bevel angle. (Bevel cuts will match the angle shown above.) Cut the ends of the horizontal braces with opposing angles. Cut the ends of the legs with similar angles.

3.   Attach the top rails to the vertical braces, as shown, using 2½" drywall screws.

4.   Attach the horizontal braces to the vertical braces, using 2½" drywall screws. Attach a pair of legs to the horizontal braces and then to the brace at each end. Complete the sawhorse by attaching the bottom brace to the horizontal braces.

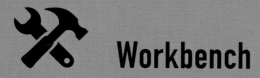

Workbench

THIS WORKBENCH has heavy-duty legs to support big loads and a sturdy double-layer top to withstand pounding. Cover the top with a hardboard surface that can be removed when it becomes damaged. Build a shelf below the work surface for storing power tools. If desired, mount an all-purpose vise on top of the workbench.

Tools & Materials

Circular saw
Carpenter's square
Drill and bits, including screwdriver bits
Ratchet or adjustable wrench
Hammer
Nail set
Drywall screws (1⅝", 2½", and 3")

Lag screws
(1½" and 3")
4d finish nails
(6) 8-ft. 2 x 4s
(1) 5-ft. 2 x 6
(1) 4 x 8-ft. sheet of ¾" plywood
(1) 4 x 8-ft. sheet of ½" plywood
(1) 4 x 8-ft. sheet of ⅛" hardboard

WORKBENCH CUTTING DIAGRAM

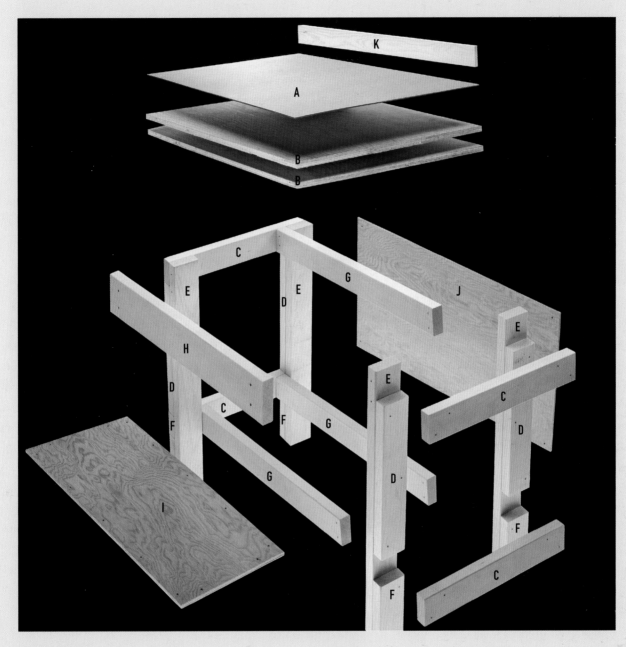

Cutting List

Key	Pieces	Size and Description
A	1	⅛" hardboard top, 24 × 60"
B	2	¾" plywood top, 24 × 60"
C	4	2 × 4 crosspieces, 21"
D	4	2 × 4 legs, 19 ¾"
E	4	2 × 4 legs, 34 ½"
F	4	2 × 4 legs, 7 ¾"

Key	Pieces	Size and Description
G	3	2 × 4 braces, 54"
H	1	2 x 6 front (top) brace, 57"
I	1	½" plywood shelf, 14 × 57"
J	1	½" plywood shelf back, 19 ¼" × 57"
K	1	1 × 4 backstop, 60"

1   Cut two pieces of C, D, E, and F for each end of the bench. Assemble them with 2½" drywall screws.

2   Attach both 2 × 4 rear braces (G) inside the back legs of the assembled ends using 2½" drywall screws.

3   Attach the 2 × 4 front lower brace (G) inside the front legs of the assembled ends. Secure the bottom shelf (I) and workbench back (J) to the assembled 2 × 4 frame using 2½" drywall screws.

4   Drill pilot holes and join the 2 × 6 front upper brace (H) outside the front legs with 3" lag screws.

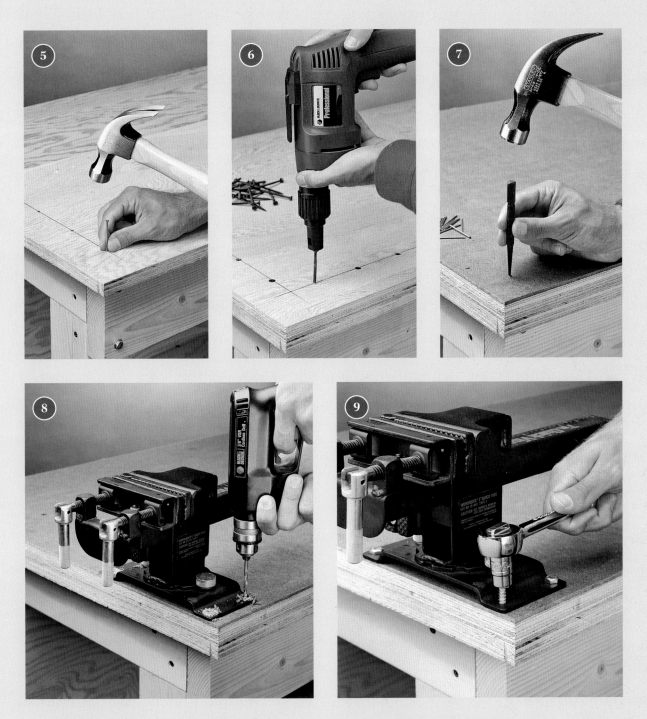

5   Center the bottom layer of the ¾" plywood work surface (B) on top of the frame. Align the plywood with the back edge, draw a reference line for driving the nails, and fasten it in place with 4d nails.

6   Align the bottom and top layers of the plywood work surface (B), and draw a reference line at least ½" closer to the edge to avoid the nails in the first layer. Drive 3" drywall screws through both layers and into the bench frame.

7   Nail the hardboard work surface (A) to the plywood substrate with 4d finish nails. Set the nails below the surface.

8   Position the vise at one end of the bench. On the bench top, mark holes for the vise base. Bore ¼" pilot holes into the bench top.

9   Attach the vise with 1½" lag screws. Attach the backstop (K) to the back of the bench top with 2½" drywall screws.

Metric Equivalent

Inches (in.)	1/64	1/32	1/25	1/16	1/8	1/4	3/8	2/5	1/2	5/8	3/4	7/8	1	2	3	4	5	6	7	8	9	10	11	12	36	39.4
Feet (ft.)																								1	3	3½
Yards (yd.)																									1	1 1/12
Millimeters (mm)	0.40	0.79	1	1.59	3.18	6.35	9.53	10	12.7	15.9	19.1	22.2	25.4	50.8	76.2	101.6	127	152	178	203	229	254	279	305	914	1,000
Centimeters (cm)							0.95	1	1.27	1.59	1.91	2.22	2.54	5.08	7.62	10.16	12.7	15.2	17.8	20.3	22.9	25.4	27.9	30.5	91.4	100
Meters (m)																								.30	.91	1.00

Converting Measurements

To Convert:	To:	Multiply by:
Inches	Millimeters	25.4
Inches	Centimeters	2.54
Feet	Meters	0.305
Yards	Meters	0.914
Miles	Kilometers	1.609
Square inches	Square centimeters	6.45
Square feet	Square meters	0.093
Square yards	Square meters	0.836
Cubic inches	Cubic centimeters	16.4
Cubic feet	Cubic meters	0.0283
Cubic yards	Cubic meters	0.765
Pints (U.S.)	Liters	0.473 (Imp. 0.568)
Quarts (U.S.)	Liters	0.946 (Imp. 1.136)
Gallons (U.S.)	Liters	3.785 (Imp. 4.546)
Ounces	Grams	28.4
Pounds	Kilograms	0.454
Tons	Metric tons	0.907

To Convert:	To:	Multiply by:
Millimeters	Inches	0.039
Centimeters	Inches	0.394
Meters	Feet	3.28
Meters	Yards	1.09
Kilometers	Miles	0.621
Square centimeters	Square inches	0.155
Square meters	Square feet	10.8
Square meters	Square yards	1.2
Cubic centimeters	Cubic inches	0.061
Cubic meters	Cubic feet	35.3
Cubic meters	Cubic yards	1.31
Liters	Pints (U.S.)	2.114 (Imp. 1.76)
Liters	Quarts (U.S.)	1.057 (Imp. 0.88)
Liters	Gallons (U.S.)	0.264 (Imp. 0.22)
Grams	Ounces	0.035
Kilograms	Pounds	2.2
Metric tons	Tons	1.1

Liquid Measurement Equivalents

1 Pint	= 16 Fluid Ounces	= 2 Cups
1 Quart	= 32 Fluid Ounces	= 2 Pints
1 Gallon	= 128 Fluid Ounces	= 4 Quarts

Metric Plywood Panels

Metric plywood panels are commonly available in two sizes: 1,200 mm × 2,400 mm and 1,220 mm × 2,400 mm, which is roughly equivalent to a 4 × 8-ft. sheet. Standard and Select sheathing panels come in standard thicknesses, while Sanded grade panels are available in special thicknesses.

Standard Sheathing Grade		Sanded Grade	
7.5 mm	(5/16 in.)	6 mm	(4/17 in.)
9.5 mm	(3/8 in.)	8 mm	(5/16 in.)
12.5 mm	(1/2 in.)	11 mm	(7/16 in.)
15.5 mm	(5/8 in.)	14 mm	(9/16 in.)
18.5 mm	(3/4 in.)	17 mm	(2/3 in.)
20.5 mm	(13/16 in.)	19 mm	(3/4 in.)
22.5 mm	(7/8 in.)	21 mm	(13/16 in.)
25.5 mm	(1 in.)	24 mm	(15/16 in.)

Converting Temperatures

Convert degrees Fahrenheit (F) to degrees Celsius (C) by following this simple formula: Subtract 32 from the Fahrenheit temperature reading. Then, multiply that number by 5/9. For example, 77°F - 32 = 45. 45 × 5/9 = 25°C.

To convert degrees Celsius to degrees Fahrenheit, multiply the Celsius temperature reading by 9/5. Then, add 32. For example, 25°C × 9/5 = 45. 45 + 32 = 77°F.

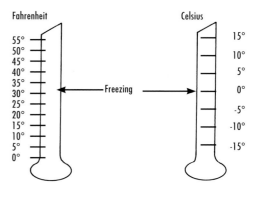

Lumber Dimensions

Nominal-U.S.	Actual-U.S. (in inches)	Metric
1 x 2	¾ x 1½	19 x 38 mm
1 x 3	¾ x 2½	19 x 64 mm
1 x 4	¾ x 3½	19 x 89 mm
1 x 5	¾ x 4½	19 x 114 mm
1 x 6	¾ x 5½	19 x 140 mm
1 x 7	¾ x 6¼	19 x 159 mm
1 x 8	¾ x 7¼	19 x 184 mm
1 x 10	¾ x 9¼	19 x 235 mm
1 x 12	¾ x 11¼	19 x 286 mm
1¼ x 4	1 x 3½	25 x 89 mm
1¼ x 6	1 x 5½	25 x 140 mm
1¼ x 8	1 x 7¼	25 x 184 mm
1¼ x 10	1 x 9¼	25 x 235 mm
1¼ x 12	1 x 11¼	25 x 286 mm

Nominal-U.S.	Actual-U.S. (in inches)	Metric
1½ x 4	1¼ x 3½	32 x 89 mm
1½ x 6	1¼ x 5½	32 x 140 mm
1½ x 8	1¼ x 7¼	32 x 184 mm
1½ x 10	1¼ x 9¼	32 x 235 mm
1½ x 12	1¼ x 11¼	32 x 286 mm
2 x 4	1½ x 3½	38 x 89 mm
2 x 6	1½ x 5½	38 x 140 mm
2 x 8	1½ x 7¼	38 x 184 mm
2 x 10	1½ x 9¼	38 x 235 mm
2 x 12	1½ x 11¼	38 x 286 mm
3 x 6	2½ x 5½	64 x 140 mm
4 x 4	3½ x 3½	89 x 89 mm
4 x 6	3½ x 5½	89 x 140 mm

Drill Bit Guide

Twist Bit

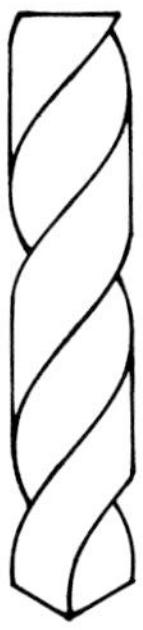

Self-piloting

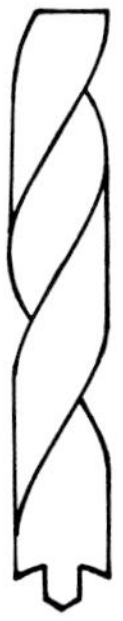

Spade Bit

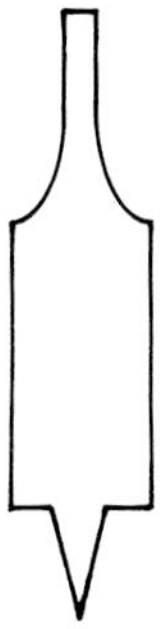

Adjustable Counterbore

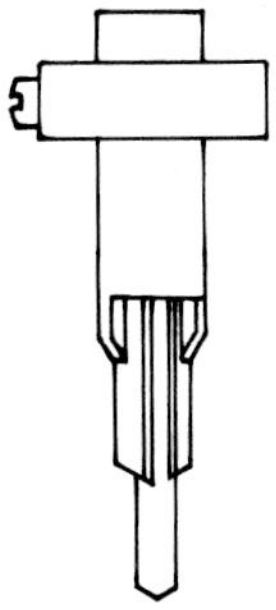

Hole Saw

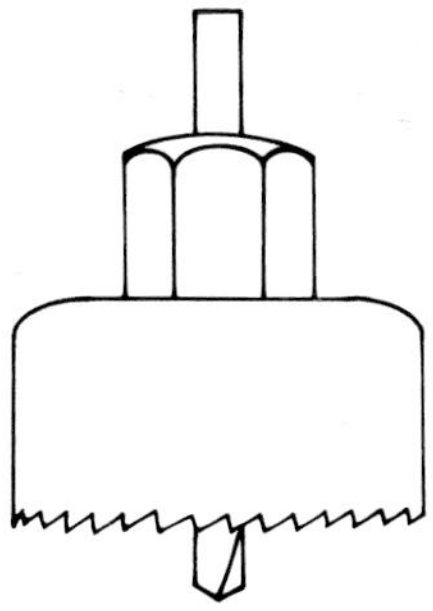

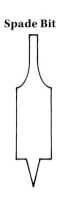

Counterbore, Shank & Pilot Hole Diameters

Screw Size	Counterbore Diameter for Screw Head	Clearance Hole for Screw Shank	Pilot Hole Diameter	
			Hard Wood	Soft Wood
#1	.146 9/64	5/64	3/64	1/32
#2	1/4	3/32	3/64	1/32
#3	1/4	7/64	1/16	3/64
#4	1/4	1/8	1/16	3/64
#5	1/4	9/64	5/64	1/16
#6	5/16	5/32	3/32	5/64
#7	5/16	5/32	3/32	5/64
#8	3/8	11/64	1/8	3/32
#9	3/8	11/64	1/8	3/32
#10	3/8	3/16	1/8	7/64
#11	1/2	3/16	5/32	9/64
#12	1/2	7/32	9/64	1/8

Abrasive Paper Grits - (Aluminum Oxide)

Very Coarse	Coarse	Medium	Fine	Very Fine
12-36	40-60	80-120	150-180	220-600

Index

First published in 2013 by Cool Springs Press, an imprint of the Quayside Publishing Group,
400 First Avenue North, Suite 400, Minneapolis, MN 55401

Cool Springs Press titles are also available at discounts in bulk quantity for industrial or sales-promotional use. For details write to Special Sales Manager at Cool Springs Press, 400 First Avenue North, Suite 400, Minneapolis, MN 55401 USA. To find out more about our books, visit us online at www.coolspringspress.com.

Library of Congress Cataloging-in-Publication Data

Homeskills. Carpentry : an introduction to sawing, drilling, shaping, & joining wood.
    pages cm
  Includes index.
  ISBN 978-1-59186-579-7 (softcover)
  1. Carpentry--Amateurs' manuals. I. Title: Home skills. Carpentry. II. Title: Carpentry.

  TH5606.H78 2013
  684'.08--dc23

            2013004053

Design Manager: Cindy Samargia Laun
Design and layout: Kim Winscher
Cover and series design: Carol Holtz

Printed in China
10 9 8 7 6 5 4 3 2 1

NOTICE TO READERS

For safety, use caution, care, and good judgment when following the procedures described in this book. The publisher cannot assume responsibility for any damage to property or injury to persons as a result of misuse of the information provided.

The techniques shown in this book are general techniques for various applications. In some instances, additional techniques not shown in this book may be required. Always follow manufacturers' instructions included with products, since deviating from the directions may void warranties. The projects in this book vary widely as to skill levels required: some may not be appropriate for all do-it-yourselfers, and some may require professional help.

Consult your local building department for information on building permits, codes, and other laws as they apply to your project.